"Ms. Pedder dispels many of the myths concerning organ donation. Her story is an eloquent expression of how organ donation is the true gift of life."
– Gary L. McMahan, National Director
Organ Transplant Fund, Inc.

"This is a story about two terrible diseases and two particularly dedicated people and how they dealt with both of these critical illnesses. One, a patient with an indomitable spirit and an abundance of common sense survived both cancer and a heart transplantation. The other, a remarkable surgeon whose focus on caring for the sick, led him to cardiac surgery and the performance of heart transplantation only to succumb to cancer in the prime of his life. The spirit of both are uplifting and provide a dimension of the human spirit that expands our understanding about surviving and living."
– Sidney Goldstein, M.D., Division Head Emeritus,
Division Cardiovascular Medicine
Professor of Medicine, Case Western Reserve University
Henry Ford Heart and Vascular Institute,
Henry Ford Hospital and Medical Centers

"This woman not only survived the most incredible odds, but is alive today and is sharing her amazing triumph with others. Nancy Pedder's story exemplifies the true meaning of strength, perseverance and faith."
– LaConnie Taylor-Jones
American Heart Association—Western States Affiliate

"Nancy Pedder was given the gift of a new heart and in turn she has given us the gift of an open-hearted story of her journey from illness to health. A MATTER OF HEART will move the reader in many ways, and will serve to promote both early detection of breast cancer and the donation of organs."
– Congresswoman Anna G. Eshoo
Palo Alto, California

"Everyone should read more stories like this. *A MATTER OF HEART* is a human interest story with a message. *The book gives a firsthand account of Nancy Pedder's catastrophic medical adventure and demonstrates how she overcame unbelievable odds. It shows that organ transplant recipients live normal active lives."*
– Charles Garfield, Ph.D.
Author, *Sometimes My Heart Goes Numb:*
Love and Caring in a Time of AIDS

"*The story of a life saved, experienced courageously and told so beautifully by Nancy Pedder is one which could be repeated many times over if only more families would respond by saying, 'Yes.' Thank you Nancy for helping to educate us about the transplantation experience. Blessings upon your donor family for the legacy of life they chose to give."*
– Peggy Schaeffer, R.N.
Former Director of Recovery Services for the Washington
Regional Transplant Consortium, Washington, D.C.
Mother of Timothy Schaeffer, donor October 1994

A MATTER OF HEART, while extremely entertaining, is also a very educational book. Nancy clearly explains how easy it is for individuals to make arrangements to donate their organs at the time of death. She is living proof that donating organs saves lives. This book is highly recommended for all readers. It will make you laugh and cry.
– Celeste Murphy, Ph.D.
School of Public & Social Science
Florida Gulf Coast University

"We do not choose on which side of the donor-recipient relationship we find ourselves. Nancy's success should make us all aware of the need to agree to organ donation. Personally I am indebted to Nancy for her inspirational effect on my career."
– Jeffrey Golden, M.D., Medical Director
Lung Transplantation
University of California in San Francisco

"This is a story that will touch your soul. It made me laugh and it made me cry as I relived the experience that reaffirms the character and strength of the most powerful and wonderful woman I know."
– Shannon Pedder, daughter

A Matter of Heart:
One Woman's Triumph
Over Breast Cancer and
a Heart Transplant

Nancy Shank Pedder

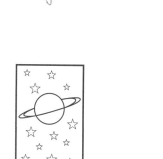

SATURN PRESS

A Matter of Heart: One Woman's Triumph Over Breast Cancer
and a Heart Transplant

Copyright 1998 Nancy Shank Pedder

Library of Congress Cataloging-in-Publication data.
ISBN: 1-88584308-9
CIP: 98-061118

Printed in the United States of America 1 2 3 4 5 6 7 8 9 10

Cover design by Lightbourne Images, Inc.
Interior design by Pamela Morrell
Author Photograph by Louise Williams

Published by:

Saturn Press, Inc.
17639 Foxborough Lane
Boca Raton, FL 33496

A Matter of Heart
is dedicated to my mothers
Mary Sheridan Shank
and
Marjorie Hart Pedder

♡

"When you walk through a storm,
hold your head up high
and don't be afraid of the dark."

Carousel
Rogers and Hammerstein

Foreword

This is a true story. It is a wonderful story. Nancy Pedder has conquered two of the most dreaded and lethal diseases of mankind, cancer and end-stage heart failure. She has put to rest the old concept that patients with a recent history of cancer should not be considered for heart transplantation. There has been no recurrence of cancer in this heroic woman despite almost ten years of immunosuppression which protects her transplanted heart from rejection.

Mrs. Pedder tells this story not merely to celebrate her indomitable spirit and recovery but also to emphasize the critical need for organ donation. Worldwide almost 30,000 patients have undergone heart transplantation, but an equal number in the United States alone await organ donation. It is estimated that no more than 20% of the possible donor pool is utilized for transplantation. Mrs. Pedder's experience is designed to increase that number.

There is here a remarkable element of human interest. Whereas Nancy Pedder is clearly the patient hero, there is also a doctor hero, the deceased Donald J. Magilligan Jr., transplantation surgeon extraordinaire. Heart transplant patients are not supposed to outlive their surgeons. Within months of Mrs. Pedder's transplant, Dr. Magilligan died of a malignant melanoma which had been dormant for ten years. A small galaxy of heart patients are alive today owing to the legendary skills of this great man

The story of transplantation continues. It does not end with this enthralling account by Nancy Pedder of her life's experience. New and safer molecules to suspend the immune reaction to transplanted tissue are under development. Mechanical hearts and cross-species transplants are escaping the designation of wild dreams. Who knows, the attainment of the life everlasting may be more tangible than in its present form of memories.

Norman E. Shumway, M.D., Ph.D.

Preface

On April 30, 1989, I had a heart transplant at the University of California, San Francisco. After the hospital released me and I had recuperated to some extent, I visited patients waiting for hearts to become available for them. I could give them my perspective as someone who had experienced a heart transplant firsthand and show them that it was worthwhile. The hard part was that there were not enough hearts available for all those who needed them. During this experience it became clear to me how extensive, in human terms, the problem was, as many of these patients could not survive any length of time without new hearts. A few of the desperately ill people I had talked with died before they received a heart. One seventeen-year-old girl made such an impression on me that I have never forgotten her. The question she asked me when I visited her was, "Do you think I can find a dress for my prom that will hide my scar?" She died the night before her eighteenth birthday—waiting for a heart. I thought, "That shouldn't have happened . . . she had a whole life ahead of her." Right then, I decided that I must try to help alleviate this situation as much as possible in the best way I could.

Soon after that I began speaking to groups in my community promoting organ donation and from that a pattern began to emerge. People were amazed that I looked "normal," and they were always interested in my story and heart transplantation. One of my goals was to show that I live a normal and active life. Interaction with my audiences made me realize that there was a general lack of knowledge and many misconceptions about the subject. I thought if more people could see the success stories they would be more willing to consider organ donation. Several people suggested that I write a book so I decided to begin at once.

I reconstructed my story by reliving it chronologically in my mind. Since it was such an incredible adventure, details came easily. To fill the gaps, I read my hospital records, interviewed the heart transplant coordinators, Celia Rifkin and Anne Fukano, and asked my cardiologist, Dr. Teresa De Marco, many questions. I interviewed my brother, David Shank, and my sister, Anita Brunner. I kept a travel journal which refreshed my memory on my trip to Boston and South Bend. My 1988 and 1989 calendars provided the exact dates of the major events. An interview with Carolyn Berry, Public Affairs Manager, California Transplant Donor Network clarified facts about organ transplantation. My many trips to the library provided important information. Several people reviewed the manuscript and asked pertinent questions that brought back memories that were included.

The result is this book written with the goal of showing that transplant recipients live normal lives and urging the reader to consider being an organ donor. Also included are facts about organ donation which should clarify misinformation and show that it is a worthwhile thing to do.

Nancy Shank Pedder

My sincerest thanks to the following people whose advice, continuous support, and encouragement helped bring this project to fruition.

♡

Ann Bayer

Carolyn Berry, California Transplant Donor Network

Kriss Brooks, OPTIONS

Anita Brunner

Jack Buckley

Elise Carlson

Katie Cooper

Dr. Teresa De Marco

Carolyn Ewald

Virginia Fox, Fox Associates

Anne Fukano, R.N., M.B.A., Heart-Lung Transplant Coordinator, UCSF

Faie Gilbert

Charles Garfield, Ph.D., Author

Carolyn Hollingsed

Monica Holmes

Nancy Huber

Penny Kennedy

Gabrielle Lapachet

Kathy Levinson, Ph.D., Saturn Press

Dr. Marc Levinson, Saturn Press

Kristin Luker

Danette Magilligan

Celeste Murphy

Martha and Fred Murphy

Erica Orloff, Editor

Bill Pedder

Brendan Pedder

Sarah Pedder

Shannon Pedder

Susan Pedder

Celia Rifkin, R.N., Heart-Lung Transplant Coordinator, UCSF

Mary A. Shank

Theresa and David Shank

Edward and David Sheridan

Dr. Norman Shumway

Barbara Sloane

Karla Steger

LaConnie Taylor-Jones, American Heart Association

Cris Terborgh

The Tuesday Tycoons

Susan Veit

Phyllis Weber, California Transplant Donor Network

Jennie White

A Special Tribute

Donald J. Magilligan, Jr., M.D.

June 6, 1939   *November 20, 1989*

Dr. Magilligan was one of the special people you meet as you travel through life. When he died of cancer, he left a beautiful wife, Danette, and six delightful children. He was devoted to his family and cared deeply about his patients. His skill as a cardiothoracic surgeon was unmatched and he saved many lives.

He was a third-generation physician; his father was an orthopedist and his grandfather was a family doctor. Dr. Magilligan attended College of the Holy Cross in Worcester, Massachusetts and Georgetown University, School of Medicine, in Washington, D.C.

Dr. Magilligan was profoundly affected by his military service in Vietnam. Like many others, he did not want to go but went to serve his country and help people. One day, while watching from the hospital, he saw an eighteen-year-old boy running to a helicopter to help bring an injured person into the hospital. The boy, who was a pacifist, was shot in the heart. Dr. Magilligan thought the boy would probably die but decided to take a chance and operate to remove the bullet. The boy lived and Dr. Magilligan decided to become a cardio-thorasic surgeon.

He touched the lives of hundreds of people—family, friends, and patients. His legacy lives on in those of us who had the good fortune of receiving our new hearts from him.

Dear Donor Family,

Many months ago, you saved my life. You gave me something very precious to you, the heart of your son. I know you were grief-stricken and it may have been a difficult decision for you to make. Please know that I have cherished your gift and it has made the difference between life and death for me.

The counselor at the hospital advised me not to try and contact you and I understood the reasons for that. You were grieving and I was going through quite an overwhelming experience. The doctors told me that I may not live longer than six months. Soon after, my condition deteriorated; I was close to death and the only treatment left for me was a heart transplant. At first, I was not going to put myself and my family through the ordeal, but at their urging and the encouragement of the medical staff at University of California, San Francisco, Medical Center, I decided to put my name on the transplant list.

Today, as I write you this letter, I can honestly say that I feel as well as I did before I had the cancer and chemotherapy that caused my heart failure. I do everything I did before and probably more. I take very good care of my new heart with the support of my family, a very caring transplant team, and many wonderful friends.

Thanks to you, I was able to see my daughter and my son graduate from high school and go off to college. I could fill a whole page with experiences that I would never have had if it wasn't for your generosity. I think of you often.

Since I do not know you and will probably never meet you, I hope you see this letter. I also trust that other families who have donated the organs of their loved ones will see this and know that the families of organ recipients are very grateful to you for giving so many of us a second chance at life.

I hope you are comforted in some small way knowing that the tragedy of your son's death has made a difference in someone else's life. Thank you from the very bottom of my healthy heart!

Sincerely,
Nancy Pedder

Contents

Chapter One

Life Before

*T*hey were happy times. Oh, it wasn't The Brady Bunch, but life was going along smoothly and I was content.

My children, Shannon and Brendan, were not only the highlights of my life but also at the center of it. They are two years apart and have always been good friends. They were constantly busy, playing make-believe games, looking at books and playing with their toys. Remembering the scenes of them marching around the living room every Christmas to the music from "The Nutcracker" still warms my heart. They would put that scratched record on the stereo year after year. I still have it among my keepsakes.

I volunteered in their schools, served on the parent club board, baked cakes for the Bingo fundraiser, drove on field trips and made what seemed like millions of visits to the orthodontist. I always said that my body was in the shape of a car seat because I spent so much time as their chauffeur. I loved driving the carpool home from school because I learned so much by getting the first reports of their day. It was fun attending their sports events because it gave me a chance to visit with the other parents. We laughed a lot in those days.

My book discussion group was always interesting, and one of my favorite days of the month was (and still is) the meeting of the "Tuesday Tycoons," my investment club. There are twenty of us: We have learned about the stock market, have made and lost some money and had a good time. I love my friends; they have always been very important to me. Never did I realize what treasures they were until I experienced the adventure I am about to tell you.

My husband, Bill, and I have been married since 1968. He was a third-year law student and I was working in the personnel department at Varian Associates in Palo Alto when we met. He has been a lawyer since 1967 and except for a short term in Washington, D.C., has been in private practice in the San Francisco Bay area ever since. We enjoy the theater, going out to dinner, spending time with friends and traveling. Bill is a sports fan and win or lose is very loyal to his alma mater, Stanford University. We have season tickets to the football games, so we have spent many hours with our friends in the bleachers.

Bill is a very private person and does not talk about his feelings. When I told him I was going to write this book, he requested I leave him out. Of course, I cannot tell the story without putting him in the picture but I have tried to honor his request as much as possible. Be assured that he was with me every step of the way in this journey.

There were six children in my family growing up—five girls and one boy—I am the oldest. We girls thought our brother was the king because he didn't have to help with the dishes and had a bedroom all to himself. He wasn't sure it was that splendid to have so many sisters, but he accepted his plight. Over the years, we have shared many good laughs and a lot of fun. We grew up in Indianapolis, Indiana and had a peaceful, happy childhood. Our Dad was an electrical engineer and our Mom was a high school teacher although she didn't work while we were young. There were about seventy kids of all ages in our predominantly Catholic neighborhood so there was always someone to play with and something to do. Many of our activities were centered around our church and school, Christ the King.

In the summer, we ran through the backyards, played games, went swimming and played tag. We rode our bicycles, played kick ball, caught lightening bugs, and ate Eskimo Pies and Cracker Jack for the prize that was always at the bottom of the box beneath all the nuts that we did not like. We squealed appropriately when the boys brought around frogs and bugs they had caught. We loved going "Trick or Treating" and gobbling candy corn at Halloween.

In the winter, after school and on weekends, we were outside most of the time running around. When it snowed, we made snowmen and snow angels. We ice skated and rode on our sled, the Flexi-Flyer. We collected trading cards, played jacks and got to be experts with our yo-yos. Our Mom taught us to sing in rounds. "Row, Row, Row, Your Boat" was our favorite and we were so happy when we ended the song simultaneously. While riding in the car, Mom kept the peace by leading us in, "For He's a Jolly

Good Fellow," "Good Night, Irene," and the Notre Dame fight song. And we were frequently reminded to count our blessings.

I always liked school and never would admit to being sick because I didn't want to miss a day. My high school years were fairly typical. I took the bus across town to Scecina Memorial and participated in some minor activities. We wore uniforms and were fairly conservative by today's standards. I was well liked but not part of the "in" group. From my view of the world, becoming a cheerleader was the ticket to success, especially with the boys. I was never chosen but was ecstatic, as only a teenage girl can be, when a very popular football player said he voted for me. Although, I had been babysitting for thirty-five cents an hour (free at home!) for years, my first real job was working in the toy department at Murphy's Dime Store in the Glendale shopping center. It was where we purchased our Tangee lipstick which looked transparent but when applied lightly tinted our lips. It was the only make-up our Mom permitted us to wear; I can still smell it. I loved dime stores and could spend hours plowing through the merchandise. I miss them.

My college years were spent at Purdue University where I majored in Consumer and Family Sciences. I went through sorority rush, pledged Kappa Alpha Theta and made many good friends. We studied, met our pals in the Sweet Shop, cruised the student union, went to football and basketball games, parties and dances. We listened to Johnny Mathis, Elvis Presley, The Supremes, The Temptations and sang along with Peter, Paul, and Mary. I read *The Fountainhead* by Ayn Rand, *The Conscience of a Conservative* by Barry Goldwater and thought I was on my way to becoming an intellectual. I thrived on meeting people from all walks of life and was involved in a variety of extracurricular activities. I enjoyed my college experience and remember it as a very happy time.

There, on paper, is my life before, in fast-forward and summarized, but my life nonetheless. Nothing about it would foreshadow what was to come . . . the journey I would take. It was simply life before, and I thought those relatively care-free days would continue forever.

Chapter Two

A Special Time

Completely unaware that a telephone call would soon change our lives, we took a trip and became totally immersed in the atmosphere of New England.

It was September 1988, and Bill and I had been planning a vacation to Boston including a stopover in South Bend, Indiana for the Notre Dame–Stanford football game. We worked hard coordinating with five other couples and all the plans came together smoothly. Because Bill was busy, I was in charge of the plans including organizing our children, Shannon and Brendan, and all

7

of their activities. Grandma Pedder was going to care for them and I knew all would go smoothly.

We decided to begin our trip in Boston since neither of us had been there for many years. I went there when I was a young girl, but I did not remember much about it. We made our way to Cambridge and checked in at the Sheraton-Commander Hotel, just a couple of blocks from Harvard University. This is the hotel where the Kennedy women had their famous tea party for Jack and it was a vibrant place to be!

Bill and I walked around Cambridge and across the Charles River into Boston. We visited many tourist attractions and walked the Freedom Trail from the Boston Common to Bunker Hill—a long walk! We visited Copley Square and Filene's basement which was so overwhelming that we didn't buy a thing. It was a two-day whirlwind tour of Boston but we had so much fun.

The next day, we rented a car and took the scenic route all the way to the end of Cape Cod. We spent the night in Provincetown and got up early the next morning for the drive to Hyannis to catch the ferry to Nantucket. We had donuts and coffee on the ferry and passed the Kennedy Compound which was lovely, as we had expected. Our imaginations were in overdrive as we thought of the important and famous people who had visited that renowned family. We hoped that we might see someone throwing a football off in the distance but there was no sign of life. It was fun fantasizing.

When we docked, we went to our hotel, the charming Jared Coffin House, an historically restored whaling mansion built for Jared Coffin in 1845. With its white-columned entrance and red brick exterior, it was just as special as we had anticipated.

Nantucket was such a wonderful interlude that we hated to leave after so short a stay, but we needed to continue to Falmouth where our friend, Martha, had arranged for us to stay in a delightful bed and breakfast inn called the Swan Point Inn. The room in which we stayed was decorated just as we pictured the original owners would have done it many years ago. It was crisp and white with a fluffy down comforter on the high four-poster bed. The "season" was over, there was a feeling of fall in the air, and many establishments were closed for the winter. We had wonderful meals and enjoyed driving and walking around the quaint town.

Reluctantly, we took our leave as we needed to go on to South Bend to join the other couples, all good friends for many years. The men were law school classmates and are avid football fans. The women have varying degrees of enthusiasm for the sport but we enjoy being together.

We were excited to participate in all the festivities at Notre Dame accompanying the football game. I had always wanted Bill to attend a football game in the Mid-West, because the spirit there is so different from what he had experienced at Stanford. I compared the Big Ten games to the ones we had seen in Palo Alto. The Stanford crowd was a very laid-back group and on several occasions, I'd seen fans stretched out on the bleachers sunbathing. From my college days, I remembered Notre Dame games as the ultimate in enthusiasm. We were intoxicated by the atmosphere. We could sense the enthusiasm in the crowds as we strolled toward where the band was playing on the plaza steps; there was a definite electricity that seemed to touch everyone. Our friend, Toni, prepared a delicious tailgate lunch. Replete and enthusiastic, we headed for the stadium. Our seats at the game were high enough to see the plays, and close to the playing field so we could get a good look at the players' faces and expressions through their masks. Notre Dame was victorious beating Stanford by a score of 42–14. Although not everyone was happy about the score, we all agreed we had a great time.

The trip home was uneventful. We settled ourselves in our airplane seats and read our books most of the way. Shannon and

Brendan were happy to see us and Grandma Pedder had enjoyed her special time with them. Everything clicked right back into place. But of course, I hadn't expected anything different.

Chapter Three
Terrible News

*J*ust before I left for Boston, my gynecologist had felt a lump in my breast. After several doctor visits, it was decided that I shouldn't be concerned but I should have it removed. I made the arrangements and went on my vacation without a care in the world and didn't even mention to my friends the minor surgery I was going to have when I returned. To my family, I down-played it as nothing to worry about. I would have the small lump in my breast removed and be done with this little aggravation and life would move on.

I went as scheduled to the Surgery Center in Oakland for the lumpectomy the following week. My appointment was at 1:00 P.M., and because it was a minor procedure, Bill dropped me off, went back to work and returned in about an hour and a half. I was so unconcerned that it never dawned on me that I might have breast cancer. Before I had anesthesia, the surgeon, Dr. Albo, said, "I will see you when you awaken and then again in a couple of days to remove the stitches." He wasn't there when the anesthesia wore off but I didn't think anything was amiss. Being a busy surgeon, I was sure he had been called to help another patient. The nurses were helpful and pleasant; they did not give any indication that I should be alarmed.

Dr. Albo is a very popular man in our community and has an excellent reputation as a surgeon. A tall, handsome man, he is sincere, friendly and has a reassuring manner. He carries a picture of his grandchildren in the pocket of his white coat and is very proud of them.

I was happy and relieved to see Bill when he came to pick me up because I felt woozy from the anesthetic, and I was anxious to get home. It was late afternoon when we arrived and the children were there waiting for us. Grandma Pedder had left dinner which was a treat for me. By dinnertime, the anesthetic had worn off so life went on as usual with homework and cleaning the kitchen. I went to bed that night feeling relaxed and relieved that the surgery was over and all was well.

The next morning, Thursday, I awakened to face the first hectic hour of the day. Bill got up first, as usual; I plugged in the coffee and was engrossed in the *San Francisco Chronicle*. It was my job to wake the children, so I began my daily routine.

"Good morning, Shannon, it is time to get up!"

"Good morning, Brendan, it is time to get up!"

Moan and groan!

"Where are my socks?" came a request from Brendan's room. "Am I having anything 'good' in my lunch today?"

Shannon countered with, "Did you see my algebra book? I can't find it."

"Hurry, time is getting away," I called.

A quick breakfast, followed by briefcase, backpacks, and lunches in hand and everyone was out the door to work and school. Whew!

Finally, there was some peace for Mom. The small incision kept me from my usual swim, so my first activity for the day was the laundry. It never goes away and once the task is completed, it simply piles up again. "I am sure the socks are going to do me in someday," I mused. Somehow there is never any urgency to begin that chore. "I think I'll just treat myself to a little more time with morning paper." I settled myself with a cup of coffee and the *San Francisco Chronicle*. Just as I began to relax and enjoy myself, the phone rang.

"Hello."

"May I speak to Mrs. Pedder?"

"This is Mrs. Pedder."

"Mrs. Pedder, this is Peralta Hospital calling. We have you scheduled for cancer surgery Saturday morning, and we need you to come into the business office before that to fill out some forms."

"Cancer surgery?" I felt like I had been hit by a ton of bricks. "There must be some mistake. Are you sure you have the right Pedder?" I said quivering. "There are several of us in the area."

"Nancy Pedder?"

My mouth went dry as I replied, "Yes, I did have a lump removed from my breast yesterday, but my doctors told me they were sure it was nothing to worry about."

"Well, all I know is what I see here on the paperwork. You need to be here by 6:30 A.M. Saturday because your surgery is scheduled for 8:00 A.M., and you have to sign some papers beforehand."

In a state of disbelief, I went to my bedroom and I sat on my bed staring out the window, unable to move. I was numb and cold. I couldn't feel anything, but I was shaking uncontrollably. I didn't question that the three doctors I was working with had made an error. I had cancer!

I tried to take deep breaths to calm myself. My mind then raced frantically toward denial. I said to myself, "This just can't be true; there has been some mistake. That's it. The hospital has gotten my records mixed up with someone else's."

I was still shaking as I clumsily tried to get my fingers to stay on the buttons so I could firmly push the numbers on the telephone. I called Bill to tell him what I just heard. Neither of us could believe it.

"What did this woman from the hospital say? Tell me exactly."

I repeated the conversation trying to sound composed.

"You mean someone just called you on the telephone and said that?"

"Yes, I wouldn't make up something like this."

"I know . . . I didn't mean it like that. I'm calling Doctor Conklin right now to find out what's going on. How can they deliver news like that over the phone? I'll call you back."

I sat on my bed for what seemed like hours waiting for the telephone to ring. I grabbed it.

Bill called Dr. Conklin, our family doctor, immediately and he confirmed to him on the telephone that the pathology report indicated I did have breast cancer. Things were going from bad to worse. Still unconvinced, I contacted Dr. Albo's office to find out what had happened and how a mistake like this could have been made. When I told his receptionist about the phone call, there was a long pause on her end of the phone as if she were in shock. It was not long before all of the telephone lines were hopping. Bill and I were calling back and forth reporting the latest. We were trying to fit all the pieces of this puzzle together.

Dr. Albo went over to the hospital to register a strong complaint about the admitting clerk notifying me directly that I had cancer. What happened was that Dr. Albo's office, after learning I did have cancer, called the hospital to inquire about the availability of surgery facilities. He put a hold on a time and, an operating room so if I decided to take his advice and have a mastectomy the arrangements were in place. Strict instructions had been given to the hospital not to contact me because I did not know about the results of the pathology report—that the lump was malignant. I did not talk to Dr. Albo until we went to his office that afternoon to meet with him. At the time, the phone call episode seemed like a major crisis but in hindsight it truly was "nothing." We recovered from this fairly quickly and were satisfied after we heard the explanation. It did not enter my mind that this might foreshadow graver events to follow.

Before I knew that I had breast cancer, I planned to go to the scheduled appointment Friday afternoon by myself because I expected it to be brief—just a matter of removing a few stitches. Because we now knew we were going to get the "news" that I had cancer, the appointment was moved to Thursday—that very day. Bill and I went to the conference together. We sat in the waiting room browsing through magazines trying to look calm. Dr. Albo was very apologetic and concerned about what had happened that morning. He said, "No one should find out she has cancer in that way."

We had to discuss what my options were to treat this cancer. I cringe when I think of how many thousands of women have been through this same scenario. It is hard to describe how you feel when hearing the dreaded words, "You have cancer." My insides went into instant turmoil while my outside tried to accept it intellectually. Now that I look back on it, I am sure that I was in a state of shock.

Although not thoroughly informed about breast cancer, I was familiar with the statistics at that time—that one in nine women got breast cancer. I was faithful about getting my annual mammogram but like so many others, I thought it would never happen to me. I knew everyone with cancer did not die, but I still equated the disease with death. Cancer is a dreaded word for all of us and people accept the diagnosis in different ways. I was upset, however I did not get emotional, cry, scream or yell because that is not like me. I was deluged because the news was dumped on me with no warning and my world turned upside down. Here I was with cancer staring me in the face—a great shock. A certain sense of fight accompanied with a real determination to beat it sprung up within me. Based on what Dr. Albo told me, I truly believed that I could be the winner.

My Dad was a very logical thinker and I learned a lot from him. I went over and over in my mind what was happening. I convinced myself that the best way to cope would be to try and not let my emotions take over. Intellectually, I knew I had to face a major problem. And so, in my own way, I tried to come to terms with it.

Dr. Albo was very thorough in his explanation but there were still so many uncertainties. For example, he couldn't tell me yet if my cancer had spread, and I knew that information would greatly determine how serious it was. Dr. Albo was very compassionate in letting me know what my options were. There were several combinations of treatments using radiation, surgery, and chemotherapy for treating breast cancer. For the type I had in October of 1988, medical professionals recommended a mastectomy, followed by chemotherapy. Dr. Albo answered our many questions and suggested we get a second opinion if we would be more comfortable. We knew he was an outstanding surgeon and decided not to seek a second opinion. To this day, I do not regret the decision to have a mastectomy because I do not worry whether he removed all of the cancer. If he had taken only the lump, in the back of my mind would always be the question, "Did he get it all?" The removal of my breast provides assurance to me that the cancer is gone. I did not want to risk it spreading to other tissue or into my lymph system.

For the first time ever, an operation was staring me in the face. I took a deep breath and asked myself, "Oh my gosh, the decision has been made, now what do I do? How do I tell my children and my family? What kind of preparations do I have to make?" Since this operation was to be in less than two days, there wasn't much time. Suddenly, a question leaped into my mind, "What is it going to be like to wake up with one breast?" I put my hand on my breast; I couldn't answer my own question.

My children were typical teens and were involved in all of the normal activities for children their ages. We are so fortunate that neither one has ever given us a minute of trouble. Shannon was a junior in high school. It was a busy year, and she was conscientiously keeping her grades up in anticipation of applying to college. She was on the swimming team and a member of the campus ministry team. As with any normal sixteen year old, she had many things on her mind. Brendan was in the eighth grade looking forward to following his sister to Bishop O'Dowd High School. He played on all the sports teams his school offered and was especially fond of basketball. Both children had many great friends, and I always loved having lots of young people over to our house.

There are two things that I hate to do, one is to ask people for money and the other is to give someone bad news. For several hours, I thought about how I would tell my children about my cancer operation. Since I was the oldest of six, I was involved with children my whole life. When I had my babies, I felt like I had already had children. One thing my Mom always used to say to us if we were holding one of the babies during a severe rainstorm was, "Don't jump or act scared if it thunders, because the baby will associate your fear with thunder and lightening and always be afraid of it." For some reason, that bit of advice made a big impression on me and I've never forgotten it. Thunder and lightening are not that common in our part of California but I was going through my own storm right now and that advice seemed appropriate.

My goal was to keep from transferring any fear from me to my children. I decided that I would be calm and straightforward. I would give them the facts and not scare them. I mentally prepared answers to questions I thought they might ask me such as, "Are you going to die?" and, "When are you coming home?"

When each came home from school that Friday afternoon, I explained I was going to the hospital the next morning for surgery and I tried to assuage their fears. I told them in an even tone of voice, "The lump they took from my breast yesterday was cancer. Now, they are going to have to take the rest of the breast to make sure they got all of it. I'll be gone for only a couple of days so it shouldn't be too bad." Neither said very much and didn't ask any questions. I was in control and calm so I assumed they were not very worried. They had no experience with cancer and had known only one person, Marcella, our neighbor who had died of lung cancer. Shannon and Brendan missed her but connected her death to her smoking.

I guess I was successful because Shannon told me later that I was so nonchalant she did not worry about any serious consequences from the cancer. Brendan wasn't concerned either. They weren't distressed, I'm sure, because all they knew about breast cancer was what they had just learned from me.

I made telephone calls to my mother, my mother-in-law, my brother, my four sisters, and my sister-in-law with the same message, "I have breast cancer." I wanted each to hear it from me so the family grapevine would not embellish it. I remembered playing the telephone game in Girl Scouts when I was young. Our troop sat in a circle and the leader whispered something in the first girl's ear. That girl would then repeat it to the girl sitting next to her and so on. When the last person repeated what she heard out loud we laughed and laughed for it did not resemble the original statement at all. I was sure if I didn't personally reassure every family member, by the end of the line they would have me on my deathbed. I tried to sound confident, but I'm sure they sensed tension in my voice. The conversations were short; I just couldn't be jovial and chat about how their families were and what they were doing

I also called one of my best friends, Jennie. We met when our little girls started school together. Jennie is always upbeat and so much fun to be with. She is energetic and is an expert gardener. When you sit in her backyard, you feel as if you are in a little bit of heaven. Within an hour, she was on my doorstep with a chicken dinner. She said, "You have enough on your mind without having to think about cooking." Boy, was she right!

Periodically throughout the afternoon and evening, I tried to imagine what it would be like to have my breast removed. Will I look lopsided? How will Bill react? Will I think everyone is looking at me? Will my clothes look funny? Will it hurt very much? It was such an unfamiliar experience that I could not reach a conclusion. I knew it was something I had to do if I wanted to live so I kept myself busy and put it out of my mind until it popped up again. It was unsettling, but I was not distraught. To be truthful, I have never thought much about my breasts and definitely not in terms of my identity. Losing my breast was not as traumatic for me as I know it is for many women.

My mother has kept a diary since 1939. With her large family, how she had the energy to write at the end of a busy day, I'll never know. She wrote on this day, October 7, 1988,

In a previous conversation with Nancy, she led me to believe that her doctor had assured her that the lump in her breast really was nothing to worry about. At the time, I was busy and did not give it much thought. I knew she was going to have it removed and that should clear away all doubts; hopefully it would be benign and the whole matter would be settled. I was in a state of shock when the news came that Saturday she was having the breast removed because the lump was malignant. It took me most of the day to recover. I talked this over with David [my brother], Monica and Karla [my sisters] after I gained control of my own feelings. I suggested we set up some type of telephone calling system because from experience I knew Nancy would be far too inundated with way too many calls from us. We could have a family telephone tree.

The sound of the alarm clock in the morning, I think, is one of the worst sounds in the world. It always jolts me out of a pleasant experience—my treasured sleep. The next day, Saturday morning, when the clock made us aware that the day was beckoning, I jumped out of bed first. I don't know what the hurry was; I couldn't eat or drink anything so there certainly wasn't a gourmet breakfast waiting for me. Bill and I quietly got dressed, and I kissed Shannon and Brendan in their beds and received their groggy hugs.

It was still early as we walked out our front door and up the steps. The garage door made its usual squeaky, loud noise in the quiet hour of the morning. I was glad I had told our neighbors, Mel and Jack, we were leaving very early or they would have been uneasy. Bill rolled the car out of the garage and we left for the hospital. It was barely light and few people were out and about. It was eerie and chilly and everything looked unreal; the lights had not come on in the houses to warm the scene. I felt somewhat detached from all that was happening to me. I didn't want to talk but I commented to Bill, "I feel like I'm going to my death sentence." He chuckled but did not respond.

Mom's Diary: October 9, 1988: Karla [my sister] started our calling system; she has welcome news from Nancy. Anita Maria [my sister] went to the hospital and will spend a couple of days with Nancy at her house. This really pleases me——that she would take time off from work to be with Nancy. My mind is eased, as I am sure all will be well soon.

This chain of events happened so fast that I didn't have much time to dwell on all of the details. I was mainly concerned about having family life roll along as normally as possible so I busied myself with routine chores. I always thought the best way to prepare for surgery was once you found out you needed it, not to linger; instead, go for it. It is interesting that, for me, it is just about how it happened.

Like many others, I had heard horror stories about potential results of anesthesia. Though I knew there were risks and the hospital had me sign my life away, I didn't worry about it. This was so unexpected and happened so fast that I did not have time to think of all the things I may have with more time. I had blind faith in my doctors and the assistants they had chosen to help them in the surgery.

Dr. Albo and Dr. Conklin [our family doctor] were in the operating room which made me feel confident. Dr. Conklin always assisted the surgeon when his patients were having an operation. He told me that way, he would know exactly what had transpired. The doctors were very efficient and cheerful, considering it was a Saturday morning.

After the surgery, the first thing I remember hearing was Dr. Conklin saying, "You can open your eyes." It is crazy, I was awake but hadn't thought to open my eyes—must have been the anesthesia.

"Everything went very well. Dr. Albo did a good job and we think he got all the cancer."

Minutes later, Dr. Albo put his hand on my shoulder and repeated almost the same message and added, "You're going to be fine. We're going to get you to your room now."

I felt a flood of relief mixed with my grogginess.

The surgery was routine and the results were encouraging. It was a very small tumor, there was no lymph node involvement, and the estrogen receptor test was a strong positive. The receptor test discerns whether a tumor is sensitive to hormones. If the tumor is sensitive to estrogen, it is positive; if it is not sensitive, it is negative. Tumors that are estrogen-receptor positive grow slower and respond slightly better to treatment. It helps determine the course of action for treatment. My prognosis was slightly better because my test was positive.

After being released from the surgery recovery room, an attendant rolled me down the hall to my hospital room. He helped get me into the bed and then left with the gurney. Bill was sitting in the chair reading a book, waiting for me. My nurse got me settled by pushing the bed tray within reach. She filled my water pitcher, showed me how to operate the buttons on the bed and how to ring for help. As she breezed out the door, she said, "Now you buzz me if you need anything." This was all kind of a novelty to me because I had not been in the hospital as a patient since I had Brendan. I was relieved that the operation was over and surprised I felt so good.

Bill had already talked with Dr. Albo and he assured Bill that all went well with the surgery and it appeared he had removed all the cancer. We talked about the encouraging results. Because I felt so well, we decided it was best for him to go home to be with the children. Saturday was always a busy day with their activities.

I was alone, stretched out on my back and I was not in any pain. In fact, I had no sensation in my chest at all. It felt just like it did before the surgery. Finally, I got the nerve to look down and gingerly put my hand where my breast had once been. I was surprised to discover the surgical dressing was so thick that it was almost the size of my remaining breast. I thought, "No one would ever know by looking, what just happened to me." A piece of me was gone . . . I remember feeling shaky. But I quickly tried to put the negative thoughts out of my mind. I was going to be one of the survivors!

♡

My sister, Anita, is a lawyer and lives in San Jose, about sixty miles from me. We have always been close friends. She is very smart and glamorous and though she is younger, I always looked up to her. She was very popular and could dress herself in the latest fashions on a very limited budget, so I considered her my consultant on everything from boys to fashion. If you are around her, you know you will have a good time. She took two days from work and came to stay with me when I came home from the hospital. She was just the person I wanted to be with at that time. We had long conversations and went out to lunch. By the time she left, I felt very upbeat.

Because of the surgical dressing, it was a few days before I actually saw the scar and by then I was up, dressed and back to my busy routine. Maybe I was in denial or didn't dwell on it as a coping mechanism. Nevertheless, I didn't mourn the loss of my breast or feel upset. I have never thought of it as a disfigurement although I guess it is. In some respects, I felt detached. I don't remember the first peek being traumatic in any way and to this day it rarely crosses my mind.

However, since I am dragging my feelings about my mastectomy out of the past, I admit that time has faded many emotions. Also, my health got so much worse that losing my breast may have quickly faded into the background. I've talked with women who have had different reactions to the loss of a breast. I really do empathize with all of them and realize that people cope in different ways. One woman said that she almost vomited when she looked at herself. Several have told me that they grieved the loss and mourned from a few days to many months. Some couldn't stop crying and became very depressed. Some put off looking because they were so traumatized. On the other hand, I have also had women tell me that it was no big deal. A friend's mother was so happy to have her breast removed that she went back and had the other one removed although it wasn't diseased.

I guess I fall some place in the middle of these reactions. Perhaps if I had been younger, my response would have been much more emotional. I do ache for young women who are diagnosed with breast cancer. No matter what age, it is terrible to find out you have cancer, a dreaded disease, and have your breast removed too. Those are two terrible things to happen to a women.

As I look back on it, I think that I was more concerned with living and probably reasoned that it was a small price to pay for that privilege. As I saw it, my choices were to have a mastectomy or die. Dr. Albo reassured me that my prognosis was excellent and he encouraged me to have reconstruction surgery, so on some level, I may have looked at it as a temporary situation. I knew that I could buy products that would hide or conceal the flat side of my chest. Since my bikini days were long gone, that was acceptable. Also my personality is such that if I can't do anything to change a situation, I accept it and make the best of it. That is an outlook that I learned early in life from my parents.

Within one day, my energy level was the same as before I had the surgery and I knew the same Nancy was inside. From the beginning, Dr. Albo encouraged me to have reconstructive surgery. He told me that I would have to wait six months but he wanted me to start thinking about it. The main thing on my mind was the chemotherapy; I could think about reconstructive surgery later. I had heard people talking about chemotherapy in the past and all the horrible images of their stories kept flashing in my mind. I anticipated being very sick and it made my insides churn. Looking at the months ahead turned my focus away from losing my breast.

Dr. Albo thought he had removed all of the cancer, so my first great worry was over. Just in case some minuscule cells had broken off and relocated somewhere else in my body, I was going to have chemotherapy which would give me added insurance for no recurrence of the cancer.

I knew a few people and read about many others over the years who had cancer; most of them are dead. Our neighbor, Marcella, died of lung cancer . . . she had smoked for many years. She had chemotherapy and was the first person that I really knew who had been through it. She had hopes of beating it, but she didn't. For me, having cancer was the worst illness I could think of having. It was similar to the dreaded polio when I was a child. I was terrified of getting it.

My mental state constantly fluctuated. I felt like I was riding a wave, going up and then crashing down with control of my emotional state fading in and out like the tide. One minute I put all my faith in the most promising and successful treatment results mentioned by Dr. Albo. And, the next minute I found myself thinking, "What if this is it and I die? No, no, don't think about it . . . think positive."

Chapter Four

Trudging through Treatments

Thinking two sets of ears were better than one, Bill and I met with the oncologist, Dr. Jones*, who had been recommended to us. He was a quiet, serious man who was very business-like in his manner. He agreed absolutely that chemotherapy was necessary and showed us all sorts of statistics to support his opinion. Bill is very good at listening to details and, although not

* Not his real name.

familiar with medical jargon, could ask many important questions and put the statistics into understandable perspective. I'm sure I would have missed half of what Dr. Jones said if Bill had not been there. I heard him, but nothing was sticking in my brain. Bill made me realize that we were in this together which was comforting. I tried following the conversation but was overwhelmed by all that was flying by me—it just couldn't be me, the one they were talking about. It was as if they were speaking of someone else. I was still in a "this isn't happening to me" frame of mind. I felt like I was on a roller coaster ride and couldn't get off.

Chemotherapy sounded dreadful, awful, terrible, but I did not think I had a choice. I remember sitting up on the examining table while these two men discussed all of the technicalities. I thought to myself, "They have no idea what it is to get news like this." Sheer horror enveloped me as Dr. Jones continued, "With this drug, you will lose all your hair."

"Not always," I thought immediately as visions of my friend, Barbara, came into my mind. She had been battling breast cancer for a couple of years. Her hair thinned some but she never lost all of it and her hairdresser did a great job of hiding the problem areas.

"Are you sure? I have a friend who hasn't lost hers and she is having chemo for breast cancer. Maybe this won't happen to me," I said.

Dr. Jones countered, "I'm absolutely sure. With this drug, it is inevitable, but you probably won't lose your eyebrows or eyelashes and your hair will grow back."

Mentally, I sarcastically snapped, "Oh, great!"

I asked the question in a different way thinking I may have misunderstood and that I might get a more encouraging response. No luck!

"Terrible news," I mused, "I'm sitting here on this table, minus one breast and I'm going to lose all my hair! How much worse could it get?" Dr. Jones suggested that I purchase a wig soon for once my hair started to fall out, it would go fast. My spirits sank to a new low.

But, as soon as I felt despair, my emotions tried to rally. "On second thought, maybe I will be the one who can beat this thing." My mind continued to debate the issue back and forth. Hope mingled with hopelessness.

Chemotherapy needed to be started soon. Dr. Jones gave me the choice of checking into the hospital to see how I reacted to the first treatment. Or, he said that I could choose to have it in his office and hope there would be no complications. I was to have six treatments and as far as I was concerned, I wanted to begin as soon as possible because the sooner I started, the quicker I'd be finished. Without hesitation, I said, "I'll have it in your office." I did not think of myself as sick, I did not want to start thinking of myself in that way and, furthermore, I did not intend to upset my children any more than necessary. I made an appointment before I left his office. Thinking about those chemicals flowing through my veins made my stomach feel like a war was going on inside because it fluttered and rippled in turmoil. Nevertheless, I tried to present a calm, cool, and collected front to the world and to my family especially.

Mom's Diary, October 13, 1988: I can't believe it; Nancy called. I was excited. She sounds so upbeat and seemingly is doing well. She mentioned that she will now proceed with a chemotherapy session. This disturbed me momentarily as Bill [my dad] was

*always against chemotherapy. Whenever the subject
came up, he used to say he would never have any of
that poison in his family. I, on the other hand, was
never much interested in any medical remedies nor
procedures so our feelings and prejudices were almost
family jokes. I never even thought of bringing this up
with Nancy. However, we are so grateful to the Dear
Lord that she is moving nicely toward complete
recovery. We will keep mail going to her.*

Although very unappealing, six treatments did not sound like many then, but believe me they stretched out into a long five months. When I have something unpleasant facing me, I want to get started immediately so I can get it over with. Little did I know what was ahead of me.

*Mom's Diary, October 25, 1988: I had a
telephone call from Nancy. She is truly remarkable.
She told me she will lose all of her hair. She has
such gorgeous heavy hair that I hate to know she's
losing all of it. I reminded her that I owned three
wigs while I was coaching my speech and debate
teams and that they were my salvation for the days
that my hair did not look good. We both laughed as
we recalled those memorable times. We talked a longer*

time today; I feel she is pushing herself too hard.
Please, God, let her be okay.

It seemed that I had a lot on my mind and now I had to decide how I was going to cope with baldness. The options were doing nothing and looking, in my mind, like a big shiny light bulb: "Never." Wearing a scarf or a turban: "What a pain, no." Or wearing a wig: "The best of the worst." Inside, I hoped people wouldn't look at me and feel sorry for me because they were thinking, "That poor woman has cancer." I admit, I didn't want to call attention to myself. Looking and acting as if nothing was going on and I was fine was my goal. I probably deluded myself, but it was a form of denial that helped me cope.

Never having been in the market for a wig before, I didn't quite know how to proceed. I had heard that the American Cancer Society had a supply of wigs that cancer patients could have. I guess I hoped that my hair wouldn't fall out, but I decided I would get one to have on hand just in case. I made an appointment and went by myself to their wig display room to make my selection. It was sort of secretive the way it was handled. A very nice lady, a volunteer, met me in the waiting room and escorted me into the wig room. She walked around the room and showed me where to find the wigs. Some were displayed on shelves and some were in big drawers like the ones in the millinery sections of department stores. It brought back memories of shopping for new hats with my mom when I was a girl. The saleswoman would pull out deep drawers full of hats underneath the displays so my mom had a huge selection of styles and colors from which to choose.

The volunteer lady left the room quietly and closed the door tightly so I had complete privacy to try the wigs on and look at myself in the mirror. This was my first clue that losing my hair might be as traumatic as I feared. Everyone I talked with said that my hair would grow back but even that wasn't very consoling to me. I had thick, wavy, dark hair; it had not fallen out yet so it was difficult to try on the wigs. They wouldn't fit over my hair so I could not get a sense of how I would look. Except for two that were inappropriate for me, all of them were blonde. As I am a brunette, I left without a wig. Now I wish I had selected a blonde one. It would have been the perfect opportunity to see if "blondes do have more fun." But at the time, I wasn't in the right frame of mind to experiment. I imagined all of the donated wigs were from women who had died of cancer. Probably their families gave them as a kind gesture to help other women going through chemotherapy. Now, I look back and realize that was a pessimistic thought. All those wigs could have been donated by women who had completed their chemo and were survivors.

Now what should I do? I still needed to purchase a wig. I combed through the yellow pages and made a few phone calls to wig shops. I researched it on my own and weighed the pros and cons of real hair as compared to synthetic hair. Someone told me that the Emporium department store in Walnut Creek sold wigs in their hat section. A woman there, Virginia, was an expert on wigs and was very helpful. I called and made an appointment to see her.

Strolling along as if I did not have a care in the world, I opened the heavy door and stepped into the store. The aroma of the cosmetic section with all the blended fragrances wafting through the air gave me a pleasant feeling. I am absolutely certain that stores must have researched that phenomena to put customers in a buying frame of mind. Pausing at the jewelry counter, I reminded myself that I was not there for frivolous shopping so I stepped onto the escalator and rode it to the second floor. The millinery section was way in the back tucked into a corner.

♡

Virginia was there waiting for me when I arrived. She told me all about their wigs which carried the Eva Gabor label and helped me find one that was the closest to my hairstyle and color. Virginia took me into a dressing room to try the different wigs so people walking by wouldn't see me. She was so compassionate and let me take the wig out in the daylight to see how it looked. She showed me how to wear and care for it. I purchased the wig, the wire wig brush, the wig stand, the wig shampoo and thanked her profusely for her help. She said, "My husband died of cancer so I know what you are experiencing." As I meandered out of the store, I reflected on what a wonderful, caring person she was and how as you journey through life, you never know where or when you are going to meet someone like Virginia.

About sixteen days after my first treatment, I was washing my hair in the shower and when I removed my hands from my head, they were full of hair. I put my hands on my head again to see if it was really happening. When I pulled my hands down again, with my face all scrunched up, I just stared at them and thought, "Oh no, here it goes." Here I was losing another important part of "me." It seemed that parts of me were just melting away, first my breast and now my hair. What could be next?

Over the next three days, I couldn't help returning my hand to my head repeatedly to see if this was really happening. It was like an obsession; I couldn't keep my hands from touching my head to caress my fast-disappearing hair. If I ran my hand through my hair or combed it, my hand or comb would be covered with large amounts of hair. It was such an odd sensation to look down at a handful of my hair.

It was Friday and Bill and I had two social functions to attend over the weekend. One was a formal dinner dance and although I knew it would be close, I hoped my hair would stay in place until after the weekend so I would look normal at the party. It was going fast. To prevent my shoulders and Bill's tuxedo from getting coated in hair, I sprayed it heavily with hairspray, practically gluing it in place. At the party, I went to the lady's room several times to look in the mirror to see if my hair was still on my head and not all over my dress. It did hold, but what a night! If I had it to do over, I would have cut my hair short because losing it was a big mess. There was hair everywhere. It also would have conditioned me to my changing appearance and made the transition to the wig easier.

In just three days, on Monday, except for a few wisps, I was bald. I had lost all of my hair and had to wear a wig from then on. For me, that was worse than losing a breast though I knew the hair would grow again. I think it is easier to camouflage the loss of a breast, whereas hair loss is right there for everyone to see and each time you look in the mirror you are reminded of your predicament. I think part of it was I didn't know how others were going to react to me, and I did not want any sympathy. Also, I was the first in my group of friends to have cancer so I didn't have anyone to talk with who had experienced it. Vanity was an important ingredient; I wanted to be like everyone else. Although I didn't stop to analyze it at the time, I now realize that in our society, a woman's hair is part of her identity. Losing it is scary and threatens your femininity and self-esteem. I have the utmost admiration for women who do not wear wigs or scarves. I didn't have the self-confidence at the time. There was a positive side which dawned on me in a few weeks; I did not have to spend time fixing my hair. It was especially efficient after swimming. I would simply pull the wig on my head and be on my way. I tried to have a sense of humor about it. The first day I went out in public was the most difficult, but after that, I got used to it.

It was not easy for my children. I remember going to the grocery store with Brendan to pick up some last-minute items for Thanksgiving. We got out of the car in a strong wind and Brendan said, "Mom, hold on to your wig." He was afraid that if it blew off, we would both be embarrassed. I had to laugh at his perception and was consoled by his concern. Just imagine if you saw your mother with no hair when you were fourteen or sixteen.

Bill never made one comment or joke about my baldness. It is hard to hop into bed with one breast and no hair, so my fragile self-esteem really appreciated his sensitivity.

My Mom always looks at the bright side of things. I had forgotten until she reminded me that she had worn wigs when she was teaching school in the early 1970s. She liked them because when her hair didn't look good, she popped one on her head and walked out the door looking like a million dollars. She did look good in them and thought they were a great convenience. In fact, you couldn't tell she was wearing a wig because the color and style were the same as her natural hair. I had to laugh at her reminiscence although it didn't elevate my spirits and wasn't very consoling to me.

Mom's Diary, November 28, 1988: Nancy called and we had a nice long chat. As far as I can tell, she must be having the usual results of chemo. I am mad at myself now that I didn't discuss the whole procedure with her before she started. I wonder if Dad were right in his negative opinion about it — too late now. My beautiful daughter has lost all of her hair — traumatic for her. She has a wig to wear and that is a big help. I'm sure it will give her a lift. But I feel for her, going through so many losses at once.

Although not pleasant, I made it through the treatments without incident or so I thought. Friends and family offered to drive me to the doctor's office but I drove myself because it was very important to me to remain independent. When my neighbor, Marcella, was going to the hospital for chemotherapy a few years ago she would never let me take her even though she didn't drive; she insisted on taking the bus or a cab. I could never understand, but I surely do now. It was so important for me to feel like I was still in charge of myself. I would spend most of the day following a treatment in bed because I was always very tired. I made sure that I was up and dressed when Shannon and Brendan arrived home from school so they would not think I was sick. Fortunately, I had very little nausea. By the second day following a treatment, I was swimming, driving the car pool, and doing all of the routine daily chores for my family.

In my mind, I told myself I was not sick, and I proceeded with my life as if I never had cancer. My children did not perceive it in the same way, I found out later. Although they were initially unconcerned about the surgery, they were learning more about the disease. They heard people asking me how I was feeling all the time which was disconcerting to them. Shannon surprised me one day by saying she didn't want to bring her friends home because she didn't know what to expect. She wasn't sure if I would be feeling sick from the chemotherapy. She thought of her parents as strong and always there to take care of her and Brendan. I tried to play down the seriousness of the situation—at upbeat times, I truly believed it myself, but I think cancer is probably a very scary word in a child's vocabulary. Also, having Mom sick makes them insecure and vulnerable and often puts them on the defensive.

This was a difficult time for Shannon and Brendan. They were embarrassed about the wig and were also frightened and apprehensive about how their lives would change. Although I tried to be open and hopeful about the cancer, they were worried.

I felt fine immediately after a treatment so I scheduled them at one o'clock in the afternoon so I could be home when my children came in from school. It was very disappointing when a scheduled appointment for a treatment was delayed because my blood count was not what it should be. I would go for a blood test early in the day and then call the nurse several hours later to see if my count was in an acceptable range. Always, I dreaded making the call because I didn't want to hear, "You cannot have a treatment today." It was disappointing and so discouraging when I'd hear that I would have to wait several days thus extending the duration of all this.

When I was first told that I needed chemotherapy, I mentally figured that I would be done in five months but with the delays, it went longer. Extending this adverse period that I was hoping to put behind me soon was a disheartening interlude. To keep my attitude positive, I would say to myself, "I've had one treatment, only five to go." That helped some, nevertheless, the weeks did seem to drag on and on and on. When I had only one treatment left, I was surprised that I wasn't elated. I felt that I still had a huge hurdle ahead of me. I couldn't help wondering if the end would ever come. I was most anxious to get some hair and I wanted to put all of this behind me.

One evening while fixing dinner, I got busy in the kitchen and hurriedly peered into the oven to check on a roast. Instantly, *whoosh*, a rush of heat hit me in the face. Startled, I jumped back and immediately remembered that I wasn't supposed to expose my synthetic wig to extreme heat. I panicked and quickly put my hand on the hair that was cascading over my forehead. A loud, deep, frustrated sigh roared from my lungs as I felt the hard, coarse, sharp bristles of what was once my soft wig. As I raced to the bathroom to look in the mirror, I discovered that it had melted and restyled itself into a mad scientist look.

"Darn it all! How could I be so stupid?" I chastised myself. "Now I have to get another wig. What a waste of money!" Today, I can laugh at that scene but at the time it wasn't a bit funny.

While I was having chemotherapy, my family and friends were concerned and supportive. I received many cards and phone calls. My sister, Anita, called every day to see how I was even though she was very busy working full-time and attending law school at night. She was there for me the whole way. One good friend, Gaby, left dinner on our doorstep each time I was scheduled for a treatment and she gave Shannon and Brendan extra attention during this time. She went to high school with Bill and has been a part of our lives for many years. I really did not want her to do all of this because she is a busy school teacher but she insisted. Gaby is always upbeat and a great one for moral support which continues to this day.

My youngest sister, Karla, is my best pen pal. When she was born, I got to hold her on my lap on the way home from the hospital, and when she and John got married, she asked me to be her matron of honor. She kept the letters coming and still does; I really look forward to them. I have a mother-in-law, Marjorie, who is a treasure. Even if we weren't related, she is exactly the type of person I would like to have as a friend! She was always lending a helping hand.

During the fall and winter I trudged through the treatments. I could do everything that I had been doing before so I really didn't feel the need for much extra help, but it all was great. I realized then and now what a wonderful support group I had.

Chapter Five
Celebration

*I*t was winter and the beginning of a new year. I always thought of winter as a cozy time. Although it was cold outside and got dark early, being inside the house with my family was a very comforting feeling. I was happiest when all of us were safely inside the house. In the winter, it seemed everyone came home earlier. I was content, looking forward to spring and renewed energy.

In March, a few weeks after completing my last chemotherapy, I developed what I thought was a cold and a cough that seemed to linger. I did not think too much about it because I had been told that chemotherapy lowers your immunity and ability to fight infections. It was also winter when so many bugs go around, however my extended cold didn't keep me from participating in all of our normal activities. We had dinner at Sherry and Jim's to celebrate Grandpa Pedder's birthday, and I did my volunteer work. Aunt Peg and Uncle Pete came to our home for dinner and Ayn (a fabulous cook!) and Brian entertained us in their home. All was going along smoothly.

This period of my life is somewhat vague but I do remember two things very vividly. Brendan and I were reading a book together which we did several evenings after dinner. He would read a chapter and then I would read another. As we continued, I had more and more difficulty finishing my chapter. I coughed frequently and my voice was almost nonexistent after reading only a page or two. Now I know it was shortness of breath, but at the time, I thought it was just taking me longer to get over the cold which seemed to get progressively worse.

Shortly thereafter, I had a day that, in hindsight, I do not know how I survived. It was Friday morning and I went to the swimming pool as was my custom when Shannon and Brendan left for school. I swam a few laps and then had to stop to catch my breath. I was finding I could swim fewer and fewer laps before I had to stop. I knew something was very wrong so I got out of the pool, dressed and had difficulty getting up the stairs to my car. I didn't feel sick nor did I have that winded feeling when I sat in a chair. I still thought it was the miserable, lingering cold that had worsened. My good friend, Jennie, checked in with me all the time and always said, "When you finish this chemo, we will have a party to celebrate."

She planned the party for this day at Trader Vic's in San Francisco and it had been scheduled for some time. She requested a special table and had invited several friends so I was really looking forward to it. After my experience with swimming in the morning, I thought to myself, "I wonder if I should cancel our plans; I'm not sure if I can make it," but make it I did. Her husband, Jimmy, took the day off from work, picked me up at my house and drove Jennie and me to the BART station. We were to meet the others in San Francisco. I had trouble walking from the station to the restaurant which was several blocks away and wondered if I made the right decision to come. Jennie could see the hills were especially difficult for me so she insisted we walk slowly.

When we got to Trader Vic's and I sat down, everything was fine; my breathing was okay and the conversation was nonstop. We had a good view of all that was going on in the restaurant and enjoyed a delicious lunch—the Bengal salad for me. It was rich but I thought I needed a treat and that was it. We had a great afternoon; I hated to see it end, but we had to get back to Oakland and our families. What my friends didn't know was that I didn't want to faint or call special attention to myself by not being able to keep up with everyone on the return trip. I was very relieved when Louise offered to drive us home so we didn't have to walk to the BART station. Her car was parked on the street close to the restaurant, a miracle in itself in downtown San Francisco, so we did not have to walk too far. It was the beginning of the weekend and I could rest and surely I would be better, I assured myself.

Because I was the first one in our family to have cancer, everyone was concerned. That evening, just as I was settling myself in my chair to watch the news, my sister-in-law, Sherry, called on the telephone. She and I have been good friends since we married the Pedder brothers. She is attractive, energetic, and fun to be with; there is never a dull moment when we are together. She is also a caring person who goes out of her way to help others.

"Hi, how are you doing?"

"Fine," I said, "Except for this darn cough that won't go away."

"I know it's almost dinner time so I won't keep you, but I'm calling to see if you are taking any potassium."

"Potassium? Dr. Jones gave me some samples and said that I may need them since I'm on a diuretic so I've taken a couple. Why?"

"Well, I saw a friend today and she said it is very important to take potassium when you are also using a diuretic. The body flushes out potassium which it needs."

"You know me, I don't like to take much medicine and the doctor didn't give me any particular schedule but maybe I'll start taking it more regularly. Thanks for the advice and thanks for calling. I'll see you soon."

Saturday I felt lethargic and canceled our evening plans to have dinner with friends, Gaby and Herb. We were going to surprise them and take them out to an Indian restaurant we had recently discovered and knew they would enjoy. However, I didn't think I could make it through the evening. By Sunday, I was so weak, about all I could accomplish was to get out of bed, do a couple of simple things like make the bed and then stretch out on the couch. By midday, I knew I was sick and thought I probably had pneumonia because of my difficult breathing. I realized it was time to call my doctor. I decided to call the oncologist, Dr. Jones, since I had been to see him a few days earlier for a routine follow-up appointment. He said, "Go to the emergency room immediately and someone will be there to examine you. I'll call and tell them to expect you." Sunday—no office hours—what a day to need medical care!

On impulse, I packed my toothbrush and took a book before I left the house. Bill went ahead of me to get the car out of the garage. I gave Shannon and Brendan a hug and a kiss and told them, "Now, don't worry, this is not serious and it is not connected to the cancer. I probably have pneumonia and the worst thing that could happen is that I might be admitted to the hospital for a week or two." (I once heard a friend say that she was hospitalized for two weeks with pneumonia so I just pulled that out of the air.) Bill thought I was jumping the gun because I was diagnosing myself and he didn't think it was that serious. Funny, how we know things sometimes. Again I climbed the front steps for a trip to the hospital. "I don't have *time* for this! I have a busy week ahead of me," I mused. But, I knew I did not have much choice. I was moving very slowly and had difficulty making it up the steps to get into the car. Pausing three times to catch my breath, I knew I was doing the right thing. I was still in control but I knew I needed some extra help to stay there.

Chapter Six

You're Kidding!

*P*eralta Hospital was a short distance from my home, about fifteen minutes by car. A ride to the hospital when you know you are going to stay is never any fun. Sunday was a quiet day. Bill stopped the car outside the emergency entrance and said, "Do you want some help?" "No," I replied, "I can make it." I got out of the car, closed the door, and he drove toward the parking area. As I walked to the doors, they slid open with a grinding sound as if they were going to gobble me up. It was just a few months ago that I went through these same doors for my mastectomy. I figured this visit couldn't be any worse than that. I didn't hesitate, I held my head up and slowly walked through them as though I were going in to visit someone else who was a patient there.

Not many people were around—mainly hospital employees. I looked straight ahead, down a hallway with vacant chairs lined up against the walls. Peralta did not have a formal emergency room like the larger hospitals so it was very quiet. I turned and saw a receptionist sitting at a desk behind a window. I introduced myself; she was expecting me.

"Please, have a seat and someone will be with you soon."

"Where shall I sit?" I wondered. There was no one else there so I could have any chair I wanted. For some reason that was a big decision, and I pondered it for several seconds. Finally, choosing a chair in the middle of the row, I sat and waited for Bill and the next step. Sitting there by myself, I kept thinking, "This is crazy, what am I doing here?" Bill and I have this saying, "Well, you never know where you're going to end up," that usually applies to us when we travel without hotel reservations. That crossed my mind as I pondered my plight, "You never know . . . ." I sat there staring at the big white door with "Emergency Room" painted on it. Just as Bill sat beside me, the door opened and the doctor on duty in his hospital blues bolted out.

"Come on in, Mrs. Pedder."

Bill read his book while the doctor examined me. In a steady voice, he said, "Go ahead and wait outside and I'll be with you shortly."

"What did he say?" Bill immediately asked.

"He really didn't say much except to wait. I guess it isn't too serious." We sat in our chairs, reading our books awaiting word on what was to transpire. I always carry a book with me when I go for a doctor's appointment but I must admit, I did have trouble concentrating on what I was reading.

The first entry on my chart was, "Urgent admit from home CA Breast/fluid on lungs." This doctor thought that probably the cancer had spread to my lungs.

After about an hour, I was admitted to the oncology floor. I wasn't that surprised especially since it had taken the doctor so long to come out and tell us something. The doctor didn't give us any details, just that they were going to observe me. In a way, it was a relief because I knew something was wrong. We took the elevator to the third floor and as the doors slid open, we walked directly to the nurse's station. The nurses at Peralta were wonderful. One took me to a room with two beds, but there was no one else there. The one closest to the door was for me. Slowly, I put on my blue and white hospital gown not knowing that it would be my uniform for the next two months.

Bill stayed for a short while, but we both agreed that he should go home because it was getting close to dinner time. The children were alone and he was needed there. I was comfortable and nothing was going to happen until the next day when my doctor would visit.

After he left, I thought to myself, "How in the heck am I going to handle this wig?" I was very self-conscious about being bald and really didn't want anyone to see me without it. I got into the bed with the wig on. When my nurse came in and saw me, she said, "Wouldn't you like to take your cap off now? You know, we've seen everything." With a sense of relief I took it off and from then on every new person I met got to know me as a bald person—"the real me," as I referred to myself. Because it was Sunday, the hospital was very quiet; about the only activity seemed to be visitors coming and going. It wasn't until the next day that the doctor on duty came into my room and said, "You have a heart problem."

"You're kidding," I replied. "Are you sure? That simply cannot be true." I just didn't believe it and could not accept that diagnosis.

I called Bill and we both agreed that it couldn't be heart trouble. At Purdue University, I had taken several courses in foods and nutrition and prided myself on my knowledge of the food groups and balanced diets. I always tried to have a healthy lifestyle for myself and my family, doing all the things you're supposed to do for a healthy heart. I exercised, watched my cholesterol, fat, salt, etc. I wasn't obsessed with it, but I was conscientious. My dad had died of a heart attack at age seventy-four so I thought I might have some trouble when I got older but not at forty-seven. So, that is why I was sure they were making a mistake. But then it dawned on me that maybe I'd had a heart attack. Whenever I thought of heart trouble, heart attack was what came to mind. I thought it was the worst thing that could happen to a heart.

The doctor said that they were going to move me to the cardiac floor. In about fifteen minutes, a wheelchair arrived to take me and my belongings to a different room. "Is this a dream or is this really happening?" my brain blared at me. Again, I had a room to myself. "Good," I thought, "I don't want to talk to anyone." Just as I had settled myself in the bed, the nurse arrived and stuck several round stickers on my chest which connected me to the heart monitors.

"This is just so we can keep an eye on you," she told me.

I had a routine hospital day that included an echocardiogram, which is a diagnostic tool that uses an imaging technique with high-frequency sound waves. It shows all four chambers of the heart in motion and evaluates it. From a patient's standpoint, there isn't too much to it. A wand-like instrument is rolled around on your chest. It transposes a picture onto a monitor that looks like a television screen. A technician brought the machine to my bedside and by the way I was perched on my side, I could talk to him as he did the test. I tried to peek at the screen but it just looked like a moving triangle to me. I asked, "Can you tell if I've had a heart attack?"

He responded in halting speech, "W-e-l-l, no. I'm fairly sure you haven't had a heart attack."

I relaxed with a sense of relief, "What do you think is the problem?"

"I don't know and I'm not authorized to discuss it with you."

I was sure he knew something but thought, "At least it wasn't a heart attack." I felt relieved and relaxed a little.

I watched television for a while in the evening, and finally went peacefully to sleep. In the middle of the night, a nurse came in with a wheelchair and said, "I am going to move you to the cardiac care unit." It is often called the CCU in hospital talk and is intensive care for heart patients.

"The reason we are moving you is that we are short of staff tonight and we can watch you more closely without having to walk so far." I cooperated cheerfully and was not at all alarmed; that made perfectly good sense to me. I was very naive, for now I know the CCU is for very seriously ill heart patients. What I did not know was that although I didn't feel anything, my heart was showing some serious problems on the monitors.

Bill tried to call me in the morning before he left for his office and was concerned when no one answered the phone in my room. He came right to the hospital and was surprised to find that I was not in my originally assigned room but now in the CCU.

"What are you doing here?"

"I'm not quite sure but they moved me in the middle of the night because it was more convenient."

Mom's Diary, April 4, 1989: I had just turned on the news when Carolyn [my sister] came home. I knew something was wrong. Bill had called with horrible news—Nancy is back in the hospital. I can't believe it; surely there must be some mistake. My mind is a jumble of questions. "How can it be her heart? She has never had any trouble with it." Carolyn repeated Bill's words, "All we know now is that her heart is in serious trouble. Tomorrow they will do an angiogram." I'm still in a state of shock. I spent practically the whole night trying to sort some sense out of the fateful words; finally I just passed them on to God and tried to get some sleep. We won't know a thing about her condition until tomorrow. Bill said he would call and let us know. What we must do is pray.

We never needed a cardiologist before so Dr. Conklin, our family physician, referred us to Dr. Woodworth who immediately took my case. He was always very dapper looking and energetic. He seemed to bring a certain amount of enthusiasm with him when he entered my room. I felt very comfortable with him and knew I was getting excellent medical care.

After a very few days, they determined I had cardiomyopathy and because Bill and I knew nothing about it, we asked Dr. Woodworth to explain it. He said, "The best way I can explain it is that the heart muscle becomes weak, loses its elasticity and therefore its ability to pump properly, if at all. It can be caused by a virus which is sometimes reversible or by other means which are irreversible."

Bill asked very good questions, ones that never crossed my mind. It must be his legal training.

"What causes the irreversible kind?" he said.

"It is possible that one of the chemotherapy drugs you had may have caused it but we really don't think so in your case because, according to Dr. Jones, you had a low dose. However, it is a rare, known side effect that occurs in one in a million cases, literally."

We felt like we had been looking the wrong way and had been hit by a train. We were stunned. Everything had gone so seemingly well with the cancer and chemotherapy. We convinced ourselves there couldn't be a connection.

There was some discussion among the physicians evaluating my case regarding the possibility of the chemotherapy having caused my problem. But the consensus was that, because of the dosage, that probable cause was in doubt. The only way to determine which type of cardiomyopathy I had was to do a heart biopsy.

Suddenly, the information I was receiving became over-whelming like a river running over me. It was murky and churning and swirling and running wild. I thought I was drowning. I gulped, "A heart biopsy? What is that?" I couldn't imagine how you would do a heart biopsy.

Dr. Woodworth explained, "In this procedure, small samples of the inner lining of the heart are removed with a tweezer-like instrument and examined under a microscope. In this way, the pathologist can determine whether a virus or the chemotherapy caused the cardiomyopathy." He paused as he went on, "This hospital does not have the facility to do a heart biopsy."

I didn't even want to know how they got the sample but I did ask, "What about the other hospitals on Pill Hill—Merritt or Providence?" I asked. Pill Hill gots its name from the 3 major hospitals and numerous medical office buildings perched on a hill in Oakland.

"We can do an angiogram at Merritt but not a biopsy."

I was beginning to feel like I was in Medical School 101. What in the world did all of this mean? What is going on here? How can one person have cancer and heart trouble in such a short time? Learning about this was not quite what I had in mind for this time in my life.

Mom's Diary, April 5, 1989: David is taking over on the telephone because he is the only family member at the moment, who can sort out Nancy's diagnosis. He reached Bill in his office at 3:00 P.M. Here is what he found out: Through angiogram they determined Nancy definitely has heart damage. She can come home when she gets rid of the water in her lungs. He will call again when he has talked to the doctor. It is 10:30 P.M. and he hasn't called. That is so hard on us when we don't hear more. We are just thinking of how poor Bill is trying to cope with his work, the children, visiting Nancy and trying to find out information from the doctor. So we will not add to his burden. I'm going to say another rosary and try for some sleep. I am exhausted and worried but trusting in God.

I was suspended in space with no support. My world was collapsing. It is hard to describe the feelings and thoughts I had when just a few days before I had been living a fairly normal, active life. Though I had been diagnosed with cancer, I was sure I had beaten it. Now this. I was not in shock because it was starting to sink slowly into my brain that I had a serious medical problem. I had just finished chemotherapy a few weeks before and now ... a heart problem? My mom always said, "Everybody gets something." I was sure I had already lived through my "something."

The first time I was scared was when I tried to walk around the unit to keep my strength but really couldn't go too far without stopping to catch my breath. I thought it was important to exercise and keep moving. I didn't feel sick, but my body wasn't responding the way I expected. The best way I can describe it is that my mind pictured me walking energetically like I had my entire life. My attitude was positive but I was shaky and weak. The hand railings looked strange to me when I first glimpsed them stretching down the length of the long hall but I soon learned why they were there. I walked down the hall, staying close to the rail because I was afraid I might collapse.

In the evening when Bill came to visit, I suggested that we try the walk again. I tried to be strong and headed down the center of the hall but in a few seconds I moved closer to the wall and the railing. It was becoming more difficult to breathe. I had the feeling that I couldn't fill my lungs and my breaths were shallow. It was affecting the way my whole body worked. The floor was carpeted and the rooms on each side of the hall were empty so it was very quiet. It was dusk and we stopped and looked out one of the large plate glass windows interspersed along the way. We gazed toward the Oakland hills. The fog hadn't rolled in so we could see the lights twinkling on the hillsides. Everything looked calm and peaceful. The day had faded into evening. We talked about how lucky we were to have such a beautiful view from a hospital.

I could tell by what was going on around me that I was seriously ill. People in uniforms were in and out of my room and there was whispering in the hall. I found myself facing the fact that death was closer than I ever imagined. I wanted to write a personal letter to everyone in my family and my friends to say goodbye. I asked Bill to bring me some stationery, which he did, but I didn't have the energy to begin the project. Again, my mind wanted to do it but my body wouldn't follow.

The strangest thing happened one morning. I was stretched on my bed waiting to find out what was to happen next when I just started to float away. My eyes closed and I could see a long path that seemed suspended in space. It was a pleasant feeling and I drifted along toward the end. And there at the end of the path was my Dad sitting in a rocking chair. We talked about our family and I remember saying, "Anita is going to be mad because I got to see you and she didn't." He said, "You should go back now." The next thing I knew, my eyes opened and I was looking into the faces of two nurses and a doctor.

"Are you okay?" The blood pressure cuff quickly appeared on my arm.

"Fine," I said.

I had read some articles on near death experiences and I thought, "Oh my gosh, I've had one." It is hard to explain but I wasn't distraught or emotional about it. It truly was a pleasurable interlude. I do believe in life after death so I guess on some level it was reassuring. However, very quickly I snapped back to reality and the situation at hand. I said to one nurse, "I'm going to die, aren't I?"

Her reply was, "I don't want anyone to die on my watch." She brought me a pill and said, "Take this, it will help your breathing." I knew it was a tranquilizer.

I knew deep down that there was a strong possibility that I was going to die soon. Once again, I said to myself, "This can't be happening." However, I had to face the facts and accept my fate. It was such an unusual chain of events that happened so rapidly. It was more than I could absorb mentally at the time. My nurse wrote on my chart that I was, "nervous, distressed, and felt weak." I wondered whether the nurses knew or were silently suspect of my fate and pretended that I was going to be okay.

My mom is a wonderful letter writer and writes long newsy epistles; she kept them coming frequently. Cards and letters from my family and friends kept me connected with the outside world. Only the immediate family is allowed to visit in the CCU so I was starting to feel isolated.

The next day, late in the afternoon, I heard someone say my name in the distance and when I looked up, I saw Jim, my brother-in-law, leaving something at the nurses' station. Jim is usually very outgoing and enthusiastic but he seemed subdued and serious. I wanted to call out to him but I knew they would not let him in to see me. He left a two-pound box of See's peanut brittle that I had fun sharing with everyone. I was the most popular person in the CCU that night!

Mom's Diary, April 9, 1989: I tried to talk with Nancy on the phone. She was so short of breath and coughed so much; her voice frightened me. The doctors have her walking around with a monitor but she is not stabilized yet. She will have a chest x-ray tomorrow. I am about at the end of my rope. I really want to get on a plane and see her for myself. I feel so insecure about the whole deal. We cannot get any handle on what started all this. Some of the medical staff must know. I am scared, worried and ready to get myself out to that hospital.

Dr. Albo, Dr. Conklin, Dr. Jones, and Dr. Woodworth visited me daily. They were well informed about what was happening with my case but couldn't offer much hope. I think they were almost as shocked as I was.

I started to think about dying. I was very anxious about the pain. As strange as that may seem, it was my biggest concern at the time.

When Dr. Woodworth came to see me the next time, I asked, "What will death be like for me?" I was especially worried about suffering. "Will it hurt, will there be much pain?"

He assured me, "There will not be any pain; your heart will just stop working."

From what I had heard about heart attacks, I thought there would be severe chest pain so, despite facing death, his words removed a big load off my shoulders. The doctor then left hurriedly. I wanted to make things easy on myself and did not want to prolong this ordeal for my family, so I requested that no extraordinary procedures be taken to save my life. This plea was easy to make because I had decided long before I got in this predicament what my wishes were. However, I never dreamed it would be an issue so soon. I got all sorts of vague responses to my request and was upset when, one morning, the Code Blue Team came running into my room with their cart. Someone was attempting to start another IV line in my arm when I complained of feeling faint and I felt myself slipping away again, sort of floating in a pleasant, almost enjoyable way. Again, I saw my dad. This time the path was shorter and our conversation briefer than the first time.

"You must go back," he said as he vanished and became invisible to me.

And then, suddenly, a troop of people appeared in my room; one was pushing a cart with equipment on it and one was firmly giving instructions to the others. My blood pressure had dropped to fifty-five over zero. They tipped my mattress to the point where I was almost standing on my head. They did not have to administer electric shock, thank goodness, for I was sure that would be unpleasant. Everything calmed down and they left the room. Immediately, I was angry because that was exactly what I did not want to happen. I wanted to die in peace. Of course, I am happy today that they did not follow my instructions.

When I thought of what had just happened, memories of my childhood came racing into my consciousness. I smiled as I thought of my sisters and me standing on our heads in our front yard. We worked for hours holding each other's legs trying to balance ourselves on our poor little necks. Prestige and a great sense of accomplishment were the rewards for the person who could stand upside down for several seconds. As I snapped back to reality, it dawned on me that my world was upside down.

There was no more discussion with me about the heart biopsy, so I put it out of my mind. Bill was getting daily updates and opinions and was very good about keeping me informed. He didn't gloss over the facts.

Bill's office was about fifteen minutes from the hospital so he came to visit me if he had a break in his work schedule. I never knew when to expect him but one afternoon he came in late and

I could see him conversing earnestly with Dr. Woodworth at the nurses station. I could tell something serious was being discussed. Bill has a deep voice and I overheard him say, "And so you are telling me that there isn't anything else that you can do for her?" But I knew when the two of them walked into my room that there was a new development. Dr. Woodworth told me that my best hope for a cure would be to be transferred to the University of California Medical Center in San Francisco (UCSF). After ten days and numerous tests, there was nothing more that could be done for me at Peralta.

My first reaction was, "Go away, let me die in peace." And then I thought, "What can happen next? What's the point, if this is so serious?"

Dr. Woodworth told us, "There is a world-renowned cardiologist named Dr. Chatterjee at the medical center whose speciality is cardiomyopathy and if there were anyone who can help you, it would be he." He continued, "I called the medical center and, luckily, there is one bed available in their CCU. There you can have the biopsy that will determine the cause of your cardiomyopathy and maybe they can help you." I did not think I had much choice. By this time I was pretty much doing what everyone told me to do. Protesting didn't cross my mind. I was able to make a decision about my course of action, but I didn't have much incentive because they painted such a bleak picture.

Mom's Diary, April 13, 1995: Bill called at 5:00 P.M. There is more bad news. The doctors are not satisfied with Nancy's progress so they are transferring her to a hospital in San Francisco. Bill said they had better equipment and that it probably will be

Monday before we hear any more. Carolyn took the call and said that Bill sounded distracted——no wonder. I was so upset, I sat and had a good cry. How could she go through another series of tests at this San Francisco hospital? It will be better, I keep telling myself but for the first time, I have a feeling that she is in real trouble. I must pray harder and be careful not to alarm the rest of the family. All I can do is talk to myself but that brings no answers.

The thought of being moved to another hospital had never crossed my mind. I knew about UCSF and its reputation as an outstanding medical school and center and I was surprised when my doctor suggested that I be transferred there. UCSF is close to Golden Gate Park and about sixteen miles from Oakland. I had been there a couple of times to have x-rays for my children before they had their braces. It is a huge complex with numerous high-rise buildings.

I can't remember exactly what I was feeling then. I didn't have time to dwell on it but I wasn't alarmed or scared. The vivid memory of a conversation I had with Dr. Conklin a few years before came to my mind. He commented, "The one thing about UC is that if you go in there with a problem, they won't let you out until they determine what it is." I was living an existence in which I had no experience and over which I had no control, so I did what I was told without question. It was as if I were totally helpless which, in many ways, I was. I had confidence in my doctors and agreed to the move but I didn't have too much hope for a cure. I thought it would be another experience to add to the ones I'd already had. They were piling up pretty fast—much too fast for me.

My children were on my mind constantly. They came for visits. I was upbeat and asked them questions about school and what they were doing. They didn't ask about my condition and the chats were stilted. They didn't generate any real conversation and were awkward.

Their dad would say, "Shannon, tell Mom about what happened at swimming practice."

"Brendan, tell Mom about Mrs. Sparling's math assignment."

Shannon would rise to the occasion but Brendan's answers were brief. The kids were overwhelmed and I could not get a good read on what they were thinking. I didn't realize it then but I was beginning to slip into the background of their lives.

For the first few weeks that I was hospitalized, I felt like I was still in control of their activities. I tried to give direction the way I always had. I concerned myself with whether their homework assignments were getting done, if they were getting to their activities okay, if they were eating properly and going to bed on time. A move to San Francisco would be a long way from home for all of us.

Before I had a chance to think about it, in less than thirty minutes, a mobile life support critical care transport team came to take me away. A couple of nurses came to say goodbye and good luck; one gave me a hug. What a pleasant send-off! Bill walked along-side the gurney as we traversed the hallways and elevator. They rolled me out the very same doors that I had walked through only ten days before. The doors closed on my life at Peralta Hospital.

The ambulance was waiting for me in the driveway. The lights weren't blinking but the doors stood wide open ready to engulf me. It seemed so large as I peered at it from my prone position. Bill wanted to come with me but I insisted he return home to be with the children. I was not afraid and we both knew there was not going to be any new information on this day. In spite of the circumstances, I was not depressed. The attendants hooked me to their equipment and monitored my vital signs as we traveled the sixteen miles from Oakland to San Francisco.

I had been in an ambulance only once before when Brendan, at seven years, was hit by a car. Hearing the screech of tires and running up the steps to the street to see my son curled up on the pavement in front of a car was one of the worst experiences of my life. I was so preoccupied by the accident and his condition that I did not pay much attention to the ambulance. Fortunately, his injuries were minor.

"Are you going to put the siren on?"

"No, we probably won't need it."

Relieved, I relaxed a little because hearing the shriek of the siren would have been disconcerting, I was sure.

It is a funny sensation to ride somewhere lying flat, feet first. I tried to picture where I was by the turns of the vehicle. Quickly disoriented by the exercise, I gave up. "Is this going to be my last trip across the Bay Bridge?" I wondered.

The ambulance pulled up to the UCSF emergency room entrance, someone opened the back door, and I felt a rush of cold air. Ambulances were lined up with the smell of car fumes in the air. It was noisy with people talking, vehicle doors slamming, and the squeak of the hospital door sliding open and closed. Like clockwork, the attendants slid me out of the ambulance on the gurney as the wheels dropped to the ground. With the EKG machine propped up next to my body, they pushed me through the emergency room entrance and took me immediately to the CCU.

Chapter Seven

It Killed My Heart

I really could not believe this was happening to me but so much had happened in the last ten days that I was starting to accept my plight and wondered now, "What will happen next?" It couldn't get much worse!

Throughout this adventure so far, I had very friendly, caring people looking after me. When I was wheeled into the Annex in the CCU, the doctors and nurses greeted me as if I were a guest in their homes. Little did I know then that they would become my friends in the weeks ahead. I always tried to care about them and did my best to remain cheerful.

I looked around, assessing my latest residence. The Annex was a cozy place—a small, temporary room set up with a curtain separating me from another patient and away from the main section of the CCU so there was no commotion and it was very quiet. When I arrived in the late afternoon, I was immediately attached to a new set of IVs and heart monitors. It seemed I was awake practically all night as I went through the admitting process of being interviewed.

Dr. Tulsky, a resident doctor, asked most of the questions while taking very detailed notes. He was a very gentle man and as I got to know him over the weeks he told me he wanted to specialize in geriatric medicine because he truly liked old people. With his patience, compassion, and sincerity, he would be perfect. I encouraged him and kidded that I would find him when I was a senior citizen. The things we say are sometimes strange. I knew I probably wouldn't live long enough to become a senior citizen, but I was trying to encourage him.

In the CCU, there was one nurse for every two patients. A nurse sat outside my curtain with a watchful eye on me and the monitors. The attention I received in the CCU was outstanding. If I showed any sign of distress, someone was in my room in a split second. I used to tease, "My gosh, the service here is better than the finest hotel."

One nurse quipped, "And you are paying more for it, too."

We both laughed as I added, "I'd rather pay less and be in the hotel."

I did not have any pain nor did I feel sick and I was mentally alert. Nevertheless, I was weak. This was entirely outside my experience when being sick meant fever, nausea, headache, or other discomfort. Since the Annex was for overflow patients, when a bed became available, after a few days, I was moved to another room where I could get up and move about. I was able to sit in a chair and walk a few steps out of my room—as far as the IV cord would stretch. For the most part, I remained in bed or sat in my chair.

Everything was brand new to me. I concentrated on learning the routine and meeting new people and learning their names. I was not happy about my situation but for the most part adjusted to my new life. I read most of the time and didn't watch much television except the evening news. I was trying to keep up with what was going on in the real world as much as possible. Bill would bring me the *San Francisco Chronicle* and the latest magazines when he came to visit me at lunch time. I didn't have a telephone which was a relief in a way because I really did not have the strength to talk on the phone. If I wanted to talk to a family member, someone would dial from the nurses' desk and stretch the receiver to my bed.

Mom's Diary, April 14, 1989: Bill's message —
Monday they will do a heart biopsy and another test.
The doctors are puzzled, but are trying to determine the cause; some think it must have been a virus. One oncologist said that it came on too soon to be the result of the chemo drugs. They have to wait for a diagnosis before they can treat her. Bill will call as soon as the doctors know the results. He asked me not to come to California yet. He was frank in his reply which I appreciated. He said there is nothing that I could do and I would be alone in the house all day. He sees

*Nancy for a short period at noon and then is home with
the children in the evening. That is their daily program.
His mother is helping which makes me feel better. I
really can see his point and believe me, he is earning his
heaven by the efforts he is putting forth daily.*

I was being tested constantly. The gurney kept appearing at my door to take me to the different lab appointments. It seemed as if there was one in the morning and one in the afternoon. My nurse would tell me in the morning what my schedule was for the day. When I had a free afternoon, it was such a relief, like a vacation. I looked at the day in segments and didn't focus too far in the future. My goal was to get through each twenty-four-hour period, one test or procedure at a time. That way I could psychologically feel like I was making progress. I could mentally chalk up what I had already accomplished. The total picture was too formidable and discouraging.

It is true, there is no rest to be had in a hospital. It was fairly clear that I did have cardiomyopathy; the diagnosis was "rapid onset dilated cardiomyopathy." The following was noted in my chart, "Adriamycin cardiotoxicity is usually a slow progressing illness. In fact, she gives an excellent story for an acute viral syndrome followed by cardiac failure with characteristic EKGs, arrhythmia and persistent low grade fever." It was still unclear what caused it in my case and the suspicion remained that it was one of the drugs from the chemotherapy.

The day arrived when I was taken to the cath lab for the heart biopsy. A few hours before, the doctor who was to do the procedure came to my room to explain it.

"An amazing instrument called a bioptome is inserted through a vein to the inside of the heart. Several pieces of the inside lining of the heart, the size of a grain of sand are removed. The pieces are then examined under a microscope by a pathologist. By looking at the samples the cause of your cardiomyopathy can be determined."

"Will I be awake? How will it feel?"

"The only thing we give you is lidocaine to deaden the area where we make the small incision. The only other thing you may feel will be a little pressure and maybe a few tugs." He explained the risks and concluded by saying, "The procedure doesn't take long and we will have you back in your room in time for dinner."

Now I knew all the details I didn't really want to know. I listened with a sort of detachment as if I were in a college lecture hearing about a scientific experiment. It sounded like a wonderful modern medicine discovery that would be fine to do on someone else.

Before I left my room, I was given a tranquilizer and wheeled to the elevator and up to the thirteenth floor. I always appreciated knowing what was going to transpire because it helped me get mentally prepared and it wasn't as scary. I was awake and they kept saying, "Everything is going fine, Mrs. Pedder."

"Great, that's what I want to hear," I replied.

"We are almost finished."

"Good."

As I was wheeled back to my room, I reflected how relieved I was that it was over.

The next afternoon, I was informed that the biopsy proved beyond a doubt that it was true. Chemotherapy "killed" my perfectly healthy heart. I assimilated the information as if I expected it, with no surprise because the way things were going, only bad news was coming my way.

Chemotherapy drugs are toxic chemical agents used to treat or control disease. They are one of the best ways to destroy cancer cells. However, they can also damage other parts of the body. In my case, chemotherapy destroyed my heart muscle by affecting its ability to pump properly. I learned when your heart doesn't work, other organs like the lungs don't operate properly either. That is why initially I thought I had pneumonia. The shortness of breath was caused because my lungs weren't working as they should because of my weakened heart.

Many friends kept my spirits buoyed with cards and notes. I call our long-time friends, Dave and Betty, "The King and Queen of Cards" because they frequently sent cheery greeting cards. Penny, Katie, and Ayn, kept my mailbox full as did many others. Penny, Katie, and I lived together in college. It is so wonderful to have special friends from "home" close by. Nancy is one of my best friends, too. She is so loyal and supportive that I can't imagine life without her in it. She and Cris called Bill frequently for updates and relayed the latest medical bulletin to Rosalie, Susan, Margo, Carol, and my other friends in the Palo Alto area. Cris is so faithful about keeping us all in touch. She and I went to college together too. Nancy, Rosalie, Susan, and I shared an apartment when we were starting our careers. And boy, did we have a good time! We developed a special bond that continues to this day. It gave me a lift to know people were pulling for me.

Everyone says my sister Monica and I look most alike in our family. Sometimes people who haven't seen us for a long time get us mixed up. It doesn't bother us because coming from a large family we answered to almost any name unless someone was calling us to wash the dishes—a big chore in a family of eight. I can remember my Mom calling, "MoniCarNancy!" Monica wrote the sweetest letter to Bill saying that if he were overwhelmed she would come from Indiana to help. She was a working single mom so that was a very touching gesture.

Another sister, Carolyn, must have had a huge phone bill because she checked on my status frequently. She and her husband,

Bob, have their own insurance business so she was very busy. Carolyn has a heart of gold and drops everything to help someone else. Our mom lives with her family in Florida during the winter. Between the two of them, they had everyone they know praying for me. My family felt so helpless because there was nothing anyone could do to improve the situation.

In the CCU, I was so busy being examined and tested that I had my bath late at night. My arm was like my mom's bright red pin cushion, the one with the dangling red pepper. I joked with the technicians and nurses telling them that I was running out of blood. The hospital became my home and I made friends with the nurses, medical students, technicians, and physicians. They really did become my family away from home and helped keep up my spirits. They were all pulling for me and still do.

One nurse named Mary was assigned to care for me the four days she worked. We had much in common including our Irish backgrounds and our birthdays which are a day apart. We had a great relationship and she was always trying to buoy up my sinking outlook while keeping my attitude positive. Mary was always there at 8:00 A.M. sharp. One morning, she came into my room with a newspaper article about Shirley MacLaine that described her philosophy on color and how it can affect one's life. Green was the one for me! So, all day long, every time Mary entered my room she said, "Think green!" I wasn't able to concentrate on it too well and I didn't see any changes except in the wrong direction. Believe me, we were willing to try anything. I love children and Mary has a son, Michael, whom I got to enjoy through her. She shared pictures and told me about his daily escapades. She always asked me about Shannon and Brendan so I kept her up on their activities also.

One day, she had a student nurse, Cathy, working with her and Mary asked her to come prepared the next day to give me a manicure. Mary commented to me, "I thought it would be good for Cathy to learn that sometimes patients need different kinds of attention." I appreciated the manicure and enjoyed my visit with Cathy. I was surprised when she came the next day and said, "I talked about you in my class this morning." I guess my case made quite an impression on her.

Celia was another CCU nurse who cared for me. She was my first nurse when I was admitted to the Annex. She always gave me a lift with her efficient, jovial manner. I never knew for sure when I would see her because her schedule varied; sometimes she worked the night shift. She and I clicked immediately and she made a special effort to keep me interested in the outside world. Once she was planning to go to the Black and White Ball which is a biannual social event in San Francisco to raise money for the symphony. Traditionally, attendees wear black and white to this event and I was eager to hear what she was going to wear. Since my wardrobe consisted of blue and white printed hospital gowns, I was always curious about the latest fashion trends. I was beginning to feel like I had been out of circulation for a long time. I found myself looking at the newspaper ads and saving her pictures of what was being shown and what the local celebrities were going to wear to the event. When she came in after the weekend, I told her I went to the party with her vicariously. After I said that, I thought to myself, "I guess I'll never make it to a Black and White Ball." Celia and I talked about books and she kept me up on what the nurses were reading on their breaks and gave me a couple of paperbacks they had finished. She is now the heart and lung transplant coordinator at UCSF so I have an ongoing relationship with her. We have been friends for a long time.

Other wonderful nurses come to mind—Anne, Lee, Jane, Mara, J. L., and Sheryl, the head nurse. Anne is now a transplant coordinator so I talk to her often. She is always cheerful, enthusiastic and I like her very much. She has become a part of my life too. There were many others. They helped brighten my bleak existence by sharing their lives with me and keeping my interest in the outside world alive. Nurses are very special. While I was hospitalized for two months, they were my friends, my visitors, and my caregivers. They asked about my family, kept my spirits up, and laughed at my jokes, as bad as they were. They worked long days without getting grumpy and they made me comfortable. They worried about my health and were genuinely happy when I received my new heart and a chance to continue living.

One day, I persuaded Mary to let me walk, pushing my IV, to the end of the hall where there was a large window overlooking San Francisco, the Bay, and the Golden Gate Bridge. I was on the tenth floor, and it was a clear, sunny day so the view was spectacular. I saw a large ship all alone, going under the bridge. Watching it as it drifted out to sea, I imagined that it was a passenger ship going on a cruise. In my mind, I could see all the excited passengers on the deck looking at the bridge from its underside and watching San Francisco in all its splendor disappear from view. I thought to myself, "There is another experience that I will never have . . . going on a cruise." I was sad as I returned to my room and sank into my chair.

My nurses and doctors noted my concern. "How am I doing?" and "Are the medicines working?" were frequent questions. The answers were not encouraging. With all the drugs pouring into my veins, I thought I would be feeling better by now. Daily, my nurses encouraged me to talk about my illness, my family, and the treatment plan. It seemed there was always a new piece of information to add to the picture. Still in the back of my mind, I was hoping that this whole episode was some big mistake. I did talk and I think it was therapeutic and helped me sort the puzzle pieces. It reminded me of the holiday puzzle I put on the living room table every Christmas. Shannon, Brendan, and I work on it every year and we have never completed it. There are hundreds of little pieces that all seem to look alike. We are constantly looking for the magic piece. It is a frustrating challenge.

Chapter Eight

Acceptance

My life-style had changed dramatically in a very short period. Gone were the days of housework, homework, car pools, laundry, meals, volunteer work, exercising, entertaining, shopping, visiting with friends, going out to dinner and the theater. All these activities fit into my pattern of life where I was in control and self-assured that all would be accomplished properly. Now, in their places, were new faces, needles, IVs, x-rays, nuclear medicine tests, no bathroom, no shower, no mirror, no phone calls, and no guests other than my immediate family. It was as if I were living another life and was completely disconnected from everything that I had done or been. I often asked myself, "Is this really happening?" I could not answer my own question. Shannon and Brendan were in school and I insisted that they not visit me every day. I wanted them to keep their lives as normal as possible and didn't want them to be distracted from their school work by coming to the hospital daily. They came to see me Saturday and Sunday. Bill made the trip from his office every day on his lunch hour. We had worked out a pattern for ourselves. I selected my meals from the hospital's daily menu the day before and always ordered enough for the two of us. I chose what I knew he liked and I ordered what I wanted. It was certainly the highlight of my day. He brought me the morning paper, new magazines, and my mail. I found out how things were going at work and quizzed him about the children, "Did they get off to school okay? Did you help Brendan with his homework? How did Shannon get home from swimming practice?" He would get the latest medical update and share it with the rest of our family when he got back to the office.

The day to day uncertainty of my situation made this a difficult period for all of them. Shannon called her Dad from school every day to see if there was any change in my status. She told me many months later that she thought that I was going to die. I was determined to keep as much bad news from the children as I possibly could. I did not want to complicate or upset their lives any more than necessary. I realized later that this was a mistake because they were more aware of the situation than we thought. They were getting bits and snatches from various sources, and they were trying to put something together from the limited information they had. They knew that whatever was happening was very serious. They were getting such mixed messages that they could not figure out what was going on and this added to their anxiety. I was the object of all the uncertainty. They were smart enough to read between the lines so they did not know what to believe. As concerned parents, Bill and I thought we were doing the right thing; we wanted to protect them. That came naturally but it was not in their best interest. We did not have any experience with catastrophic illness and were just operating by trial and error. At night, I thought of my children—my babies—and I didn't want to leave them yet.

It would have been better if we had given them a more detailed explanation. This was a family crisis, and we should have given them straightforward information. I had done that when I told them about my cancer operation, but Bill and I were also overwhelmed and not thinking as clearly as we might normally be. We should have been their main source of information so they wouldn't have had to sort through comments and actions of others. Everyone was trying to help and we appreciated that so very much. It really contributed to our success in getting through the whole ordeal. Knowing that people cared was part of the cure.

Shannon went to her Junior Prom while I was hospitalized. Fortunately, her grandmother and I had already helped her select her dress. It was a beautiful shade of blue with a full skirt and perfect for her. I was looking forward to the evening almost as much as she was and had planned on taking tons of photographs for her grandmothers. I was very disappointed not to be able to see her off on this special occasion. This was the first important event that I was going to miss and I was unhappy about it. I remembered the excitement revolving around formal dances when I was in high school; more than half the fun was the anticipation and getting dressed. My little sisters watched as a blue jean-clad teenager became a princess and when the doorbell rang, they peeked around the corner so they could see my date. Off we would go into the magic of the night. I wanted to be part of Shannon's first formal dance and wanted this to be a special night for her. I almost cried every time I thought about missing this, but I did not tell Bill how I was feeling because he had enough on his mind.

Grandma Pedder came to our house and helped Shannon get dressed and get her hair fixed for the dance. She also made sure pictures were taken and gave Shannon the last-minute encouragements she needed for this big evening. I will be forever grateful to her date because he drove her from Oakland to San Francisco to see me in the hospital before they started their evening festivities. Shannon walked into my room in the early evening and she looked like a princess. They didn't stay very long but that handsome young couple was the hit of the CCU that night. I was able to give my daughter a hug and tell her how beautiful she looked after all.

Brendan didn't say much on his visits but I understood. It is difficult for children to see a sick parent and even more so when she is in intensive care, hooked up to all sorts of scary-looking things. I know he was puzzled and overwhelmed. He submitted the following poem for a school assignment and I think it sums up how he was feeling.

Brendan's Poem

Nothing is worse than stress
Tests make me want to cry
My desk is a mess
I don't even want to try

Science is the pits
It leads into a trap
I want to rip my papers into bits
During class I want to nap

Understanding novels is a bore
Computers are a drag
I don't want to do this anymore
This is not my bag

If this doesn't make any sense
See me in the office

It took me a while to catch on to the titles of my caregivers, especially the doctors. At first, it did not dawn on me that because I was in a hospital affiliated with a medical school, some of the myriad of people coming to see me were students. There were several cardiology fellows who visited me regularly. Fellows are doctors who have completed medical school, a residency program, and are now doing extra years in their speciality area.

Doctor Kwasman was a cardiac fellow. He was a handsome young man, very friendly and upbeat. He talked to me several times about an experimental drug therapy that might improve my condition. It gave me a smidgen of hope. I signed all the consent forms and was ready to start when Dr. Kwasman returned and said, "We can't do it because of your age."

"What?"

"The company that makes the drug has withdrawn permission because you are still in the childbearing age range."

I think he was more disappointed than I. I assumed there must be some risk and believe me, I did not want more side-effect problems. But still, another avenue of hope had shut down.

It became increasingly clear to me that I was extremely ill, and the options open for a cure were very limited. I was totally dependent on IV drugs to keep my heart pumping. I don't know what was going on behind the scenes but step by step, they were letting me know that my life would never be the same. The doctors, and I had many, couldn't say precisely what was going to happen. They told me that I might not be able to leave my home and certainly could not expect to do all the things I had been used to doing—even the most routine chores like grocery shopping. It might be that I would have difficulty walking across the room; they just didn't know for sure. That news absolutely stunned me. How could I adjust to a life like that? It would be horrible. Again, I had a sense of disbelief and, to this day, I have a feeling that it happened to someone else. Now, I'm wondering if that wasn't a coping mechanism.

For months, my brother, David, and his wife, Theresa, looked forward to a twenty-fifth wedding anniversary trip to California. The detailed arrangements were all in place. Looking forward to their visit, I was anxious to show Theresa around because she had never been to California. Also, I had planned, in my mind, a dinner party to introduce them to our friends. I was very disappointed to be hospitalized when they came for their special vacation. Bill got permission for them to visit me in the CCU. Although I was excited about their visit, I didn't want them to see me looking like I was on death's door. They had not seen me since I had lost all my hair so I knew my appearance and especially the baldness would be a shock for them.

For two days, I contemplated how I would prepare for their visit. It seems silly now because they knew I was very sick and probably didn't expect me to look good. Because I am the oldest sibling in my family, I always thought I should be strong and though I was sliding toward death, I was determined to put on a good front. My reasoning process was definitely distorted. Down deep, I think I didn't want them to remember me looking so feeble. Although not aware of it, perhaps I was preparing them and me for the inevitable.

Mary and I had discussed our timeline for getting me ready. Although unspoken, we both knew it was going to take tremendous energy on my part. She was great and continually tried to make me feel confident. We were to begin preparing about a half-hour before they were to arrive. We thought it best for me to stay in bed until they arrived at the CCU desk. I was so weak and had so little energy that I couldn't get motivated. It was frustrating because my mind pictured me getting up but my body just wouldn't cooperate. Mary walked over to the closet, took the wig out of the plastic bag and helped me put it on; it was the first time I had worn it since I had been admitted to the hospital. She passed me the cosmetic pouch and I reached in for the eyeliner—my eyelashes were almost gone by this time. Without a mirror, I put a little liner on my lids and lipstick on my lips. This small bit of activity took so much effort and completely depleted my energy reserve. The front desk notified Mary that my guests had arrived. Mary helped me get in my chair (I didn't want to be in bed when they arrived), stood back and said, "You look fine."

Bill, David, and Theresa arrived a few seconds later and I could tell by the look on my brother's face that I did not look fine. His eyes filled with tears as he tried to act normal. He told me recently that my wig was askew, the eyeliner was way too dark, and the lipstick was not on straight. He said my appearance combined with the fact that I looked very weak and was hooked up to monitors and IVs was almost too much for him.

David is the rock of our family; he and I are the oldest siblings in our family. We were born eighteen months apart and we are close friends. Our family was starved for information about me; they knew when I was moved to UCSF that things were more serious than they had initially thought. David was anxious to see for himself exactly what was happening. In the elevator on the way up to my room, he was apprehensive and his heart was beating fast. He asked himself, "How am I going to handle this, what am I going to say?"

When he and Theresa entered the strange world of the CCU, David immediately noticed all the equipment and reminded himself that it was life saving. Mary greeted them, introductions were made, and she quietly slipped from the room. They were both shocked at my appearance and didn't think I looked like "me" at all. They thought that I was tied in the chair but I wasn't. It was just that I was so thin and weak that I couldn't sit up straight so I was slumping over. It was hard for me to talk because of the shortness of breath so they stayed for about fifteen minutes and we chatted about their drive up Highway One and their visit to Carmel. Because our family had driven that route several times before I could picture the beautiful scenery they experienced. David told me later that it was hard for him to keep his mind on the conversation and the whole experience was emotionally draining for him. They left feeling very helpless.

Mary popped right into the room, "How did it go?"

"Okay."

She helped me get out of the chair and back in bed. The wig had been very uncomfortable so I was happy to take it off and have her return it to the small closet in the corner of the room. I was totally exhausted.

Mom's Diary, April 22, 1989: We have been on pins and needles waiting to get a firsthand report on Nancy from David and Theresa. We all felt that we were getting so little information and were happy that they decided to go ahead with their trip to the Bay Area. We hoped that it would calm our fears. They called this afternoon to tell me about their visit with her and their reactions. When David first saw her, he burst out crying, the shock of seeing her so helpless, thin, and with no hair was too much. I'm sure he felt he was looking at death for the first time in his life and it was his sister.

They spent about fifteen minutes with her in the CCU. She is very short of breath, has a tube into her heart and she is very weak, but she was sitting in a chair. She insists she will get better. The doctors are experimenting with medicines trying to stabilize her. Can they save her?

Bill put aside his own troubles and took some time from work to spend with David and Theresa. He was trying to control his own fears and those of the children, but he still could think of us and try to allay our fears. It showed me very clearly what a great husband and father he is. When I saw the whole picture, I realized then that Nancy's life or death is in God's hands now. I was consoled knowing both families were standing in the wings asking Him for Nancy's best interests which only He could see. Now it is bed time for me. I have to keep up my courage and try to fight off depression. I am trying to keep up my prayers——say as many as I can. It helps to keep me sane and renews my trust in the Lord.

One day, my nurse said to me enthusiastically, "Do you see that man walking down the hall? He is our first heart transplant patient, Carlos." She explained that he had been in the hospital for quite some time. He was staying in a room at the end of the unit, which sounded to me like it was similar to living in quarantine.

I asked, "What does he do all day?"

"Oh, he listens to the radio and things like that."

Within myself, I had not accepted long-term hospitalization so I thought, "How absolutely boring!"

As I saw him disappear down the hall wearing his mask, pushing his IV pole, and walking with his physical therapist, I immediately said to myself, "I would never have a heart transplant." I remembered all of the television coverage of the first transplant recipients back in the late 1960s when Dr. Christian Barnaard and Dr. Norman Shumway were in the news with their groundbreaking surgery. Dr. Shumway did the first heart transplant in the United States at Stanford University and is one of my heroes. There was one man in my home state, Indiana, who was rolled out on his front porch for the television cameras every year on the anniversary of his heart transplant. He was in a wheelchair and had a large oxygen tank by his side. I really didn't focus in on these events insofar as my life was concerned, but it is cemented in my mind—the fact that I could never accept that life style.

I was young by heart disease standards and somewhat unique in having had cancer also, so I received a lot of attention. Dr. Tulsky visited me often and when he came in to chat one day he mentioned somewhat casually, "You may want to think of having a heart transplant sometime, perhaps in a year or so." He added, "It may be something to contemplate seriously."

I said, "I am definitely not interested." And I took his idea so lightly that I did not even mention it to Bill because I had absolutely no intention of following through with such a suggestion. The previous examples I had seen were enough for me, so I put that idea right out of my mind.

♡

The days passed slowly one by one; my heart continued to deteriorate. I felt weaker and could do less and less. In fact, I was bedridden for all practical purposes. On one of his regular visits, Dr.Tulsky told me, "You have a 50 percent chance of living one year." Finally, I accepted the fact that I was going to die. I had already had two near-death experiences in the past few weeks and I was at peace with it. I felt that I had a good life and had done many things. I knew it would be a difficult adjustment for Bill, but I also knew that his life would go on and I even told myself he would probably remarry. Also, Shannon and Brendan were young teenagers now and were on their way to becoming capable and strong adults. I didn't want to leave them. I had enjoyed every one of their "stages" including the "terrible twos" (which really were not terrible). My dreams were to participate in the happy celebrations of their lives including graduations, weddings, and the births of their children—perhaps this was not meant to be. They had never caused us any trouble, and I knew they would miss me—but I felt certain they could go on without me.

This was a distressful time for Bill. One lunch time when he came to see me, he said, "I wasn't going to tell you this but since the results were okay, I will."

My heart sank, "What?"

"I had chest pains at work this morning so I went to Dr. Conklin's office. I was sure I was having a heart attack and was afraid to drive so I had my secretary take me."

I sat there, propped up in my bed just staring at him. This was beyond belief—incomprehensible at that moment.

"I had an EKG and Dr. Conklin said it was stress. I didn't have a heart attack." Dr. Conklin had been following the unfolding of this nightmare and knew what our family was experiencing.

With extreme relief, I tried to joke, "Oh, sympathy pains." Instantly, Shannon and Brendan leaped into my mind. Dad having a heart attack would be too much. It would be dreadful for them to have two incapacitated parents.

In about two minutes, the elevator of my emotions bounced off the basement floor and headed up again. Bill hid the turmoil I know he was experiencing. I could see that it was difficult for him to juggle his law practice, run the household, keep up with the children, keep family and friends informed, visit me daily in San Francisco and try to keep all of our spirits from falling out of the bottom of the barrel. Added to all of this was the frustration that there truly was nothing anyone could do. It made me happy that friends were thinking of him too. His wonderful mother was a tremendous support to him and helped in any way she could.

Religion has always been an important part of my life. Having faith and putting my trust in God is like comfort food for the soul. The prayers of family and friends of all denominations gave me the inner strength to survive my medical nightmare.

I'm sure the emotional process of accepting death is different for every individual. Explaining in hindsight what and how I was thinking about my own death is difficult, especially since I am presently living a full life and delighted to be alive. I believe I will be in a better place when I die which makes the prospect of leaving this life more acceptable. At the time, there was not much hope I would live very long. No choices or options were presented. For example, no one said, "If you take this medicine, live this life style or have this operation, your heart will get better." So, there really wasn't anything I could do about getting well.

I find it very interesting that, when faced with death, I could let go of so many things. Those things I once thought were so meaningful, now didn't matter. It wasn't that I didn't care about them, but they were irrelevant. It was not a conscious effort; it just happened. For example, my material possessions . . . I always thought I wanted this person to have this and that person to have something else. But, when it got right down to it, those things were not important. I didn't worry about whether Shannon and Brendan had done their homework like I did when I was first admitted to the hospital. It simply wasn't my problem anymore.

Future plans meant nothing to me; I had a feeling of complete detachment. I really looked forward to a peaceful end. My emotional energy was slipping away. I cared about my friends and family and what they were doing but it was as if I were taking myself out of the picture of my life as it had been before I was sick. The fight to keep going dissipated and a sense of acceptance set into my being. I have difficulty describing it to people now, especially when I tell them, "Dying isn't that bad."

When I read my medical records later, I noted there was an entry that indicated I seemed depressed. I'm sure I was feeling pretty low although I did not cry or get scared. The fear of the unknown was not present because I was sure my heart would just give up and stop pumping. The concerns of wondering "How am I going to die?" and "Where am I going to die?" were not there. I would be right there in the CCU and my heart would just give up and stop pumping. At least that was what my brain told me. There was no intellectual versus emotional battle going on. It seemed that everything was synchronized. Was this denial or a coping mechanism? I do not know.

By the way I feel today, I can't imagine being in that frame of mind. I did wonder if I would be alone when I slipped away and I wondered what they would do to try and save me. However, I never asked. One thing that kept me from being too emotional about it was that someone was in my room all the time so there really wasn't much time for meditation. In the CCU, they watch and measure your vital signs constantly. Early in my hospital stay, Bill and I discussed some aspects of my will, but except for Dr. Magilligan, I never talked to anyone about my death. I knew people were uncomfortable discussing it so I kept my own counsel.

The turning point was the mention of the heart transplant. Although I initially was opposed to it for me, I believe it opened the window of hope just a crack. The enthusiasm of my doctors pried it open even more.

Chapter Nine

She Is Not Responding

A few days later, Dr. Tulsky came into my room over the noon hour to talk to Bill and me. He was carrying a clipboard and sat in a chair under the window. We could tell by his demeanor that this was going to be a serious discussion but we had no clue what he was going to say. Bill had brought me a hamburger and a chocolate milkshake (I love chocolate!) which was my treat for the week, and a break from the cardiac diet of the hospital. I had gotten special permission to have the hamburger (with everything on it!), and I looked forward to it all morning and couldn't wait for it and the milkshake to arrive with Bill. I do not know how Dr. Tulsky drew the lot of having to give us the bad news but I've often thought what a professional, caring way he delivered it. He said, "The only possible 'treatment' [I thought that was a little understated!] you have left to try that may cure you is a heart transplant." I can't say I was stunned because he had previously mentioned it. What could I say? Absolutely nothing!

Bill asked many pertinent questions. "Let me ask you bluntly, are you telling us that if she doesn't have this transplant she will die?"

That was a hard one to answer but he said, "Her condition is significantly worsening as the days go by." He quoted results from the thousands of tests I was having regularly like my ejection fraction which was down to under 13 percent. The ejection fraction test measures how the heart functions or pumps; a normal reading would be 60 percent.

"What are her survival chances if she has a transplant?" Again, more statistics.

"How do you get the hearts?"

"The California Transplant Donor Network, right here in San Francisco, coordinates that for the hospitals in this area. It is a federally designated organ procurement organization that is a nonprofit, public benefit corporation. The Donor Network coordinates organ recovery and distribution and educates health care professionals and the public about organ and tissue donation and transplantation. After she qualifies, her name will be put on a list. The first heart that matches when she is at the top of the list is offered to her. The hearts come from cadaver donors who are brain dead. That means there are no brain waves. A person who is brain dead is permanently unable to think, breathe, see, hear, or feel. Most of the hearts come from teenagers who have been in motorcycle and bicycle accidents. If a heart becomes available for her, the heart transplant surgeon, Dr. Magilligan, will go and look at it to see if he thinks it is a good match. Then he will remove it and bring it to UCSF to be transplanted."

Trying to sort out the logistics of this scene, I inquired, "How will the heart get here?"

"When we get a call informing us that a suitable matching heart is available, Dr. Magilligan and an operating room technician will go and get it. If it is close, they will go in an ambulance or have a police escort. If it is farther away, they will go by plane out of the San Francisco airport.

"What about a helicopter?"

"There is no place convenient to the medical center to land a helicopter." Although I hadn't thought about it before, I found that interesting.

"We have an arrangement with some companies where we rent their corporate Lear jets to make the trip. Transportation waits for them at their destination and rushes them to the hospital where the donor is located. The vehicle waits right there and when the organ is procured, rushes them back to the airport. UCSF has two vans that are always at the San Francisco airport. When the plane lands, one of them picks up the doctor, the technician, and the organ and drives immediately to UCSF. And yes, what you've heard about the organs coming in the igloo coolers is correct; they are the perfect size."

It sounded like quite a drama to me.

"What if it is across the Golden Gate Bridge or the Bay Bridge and it is commute time?"

"Don't worry about that; we will work it out."

For some reason, the commute hour on the bridge really bothered me and recurred on my question list. I was anxious about how my new heart and I were going to get together. Arriving in the operating room to discover the heart had been caught in a traffic jam was my idea of a disaster.

"We plan and review every detail; retrieving the heart is fine-tuned to the minute so there won't be any snafus."

He patiently went over the details again. Of course, I could see he was trying to ease my concern and didn't want me to think about things that were completely out of my control. Amazingly, I didn't fret about the particulars too much—except the bridge.

Initially, I did not see much of Dr. Magilligan. I'm sure he was involved in discussions about my treatment all along and especially when the transplant became a possibility. When he did visit, he stood very erect at the end of my bed looking straight at me. He always had a folder in his hand that he carried by his side. He had been a marine during the Vietnam War and impressed me as very organized. Discussions I had with him on various topics made me realize that he was a very informed, smart man. Bill and I liked him immediately. He thought families were very important. I felt a kinship with him when I learned of his Irish background and his six children—five girls and one boy—just like the family in which I was raised.

Although at this time I was simply learning about heart transplantation and had not decided to do it, I tried to put myself vaguely in the picture as I sat in my bed listening. Somehow, it was comforting to know he would screen my potential new heart first but I worried that he might be too tired to do the surgery after traveling to get the heart. He would be involved from the moment they got the call that a heart was available. My feelings were mixed, swinging from one extreme to the other. This was something I had never considered in my wildest thoughts would ever be a discussion about me. I think a little hope was seeping into my brain.

"Do you use anyone's heart that says he wants to be a donor?" I asked Dr. Tulsky.

Patiently, Dr. Tulsky explained, "The donor cannot have had any heart disease, systemic illness, or any serious injury to the chest which may have affected the heart. The screening of the heart is a very careful, thorough procedure."

"How long will I live with a new heart?"

"Of course, no one knows for sure but the survival rate is 85 percent the first year, and Dr. Magilligan's rate is a little higher. The longest living heart transplant patient has had his heart for almost twenty years."

"Well, there is a smidgen of hope." My thoughts were swinging back and forth, so I immediately put myself in that man's category. And, for the moment, I adopted the attitude that the sky is the limit.

"How long will she have to wait?" Bill inquired.

"The average wait is about three months, but we never really know."

I looked at the calendar on the wall and thought to myself, "No way can I sit in this hospital bed for three months."

"Is this dangerous surgery? I guess I'm asking does it really work and is it worth it, considering all she is going to have to go through?"

Dr. Tulsky immediately responded, "A heart transplant is no longer considered an experiment. It is an acceptable treatment for many people with end-stage heart disease." "End-stage? . . . end-stage?" I was thinking—not too encouraging!

I could see he was choosing his answers carefully. He wanted to be encouraging but there was the risk that it would not be successful. I was getting mixed messages, although I did not believe he was hiding anything.

I participated mentally as the questions and answers flew by me but it was as if they were talking about someone else, not me. This was like a flashback. I had participated in this same scene several months ago when Bill, my oncologist, and I discussed the chemotherapy. Now, I just sat in my chair listening as my hamburger sat in my lap getting cold. I felt like I had a brick in my stomach. Somehow, the hamburger didn't look that good anymore.

The conversation with Dr. Tulsky about the heart transplant was strange in a way I have difficulty describing. I participated knowing we were talking about me but it was as if I was learning about transplantation in an academic setting. There I was listening to a lecture and not thinking of it as something that would happen to me anytime soon—if ever. It seemed to be a modern medical miracle; everything sounded fascinating and logical—there was my dad's way of thinking again.

Shannon came to visit me this day, my twenty-fourth in the hospital, because her school had a holiday. Dr. Tulsky arrived shortly thereafter and said he wanted to talk to Bill and me and he suggested we might want to have Shannon wait outside. By what was happening, I knew we were going to be involved in some sort of serious discussion. I was glad we asked Shannon to leave because we had tried to shelter both children from the gravity of the situation until we could sort it out for ourselves. I truly had no idea what he was going to say to us. She sat outside the room at the nurse's table with only a heavy curtain between her and us and unbeknown to us heard all about the potential heart transplant. It was an unfortunate situation all the way around. The nurses knew what was transpiring and could see that she was upset so they brought her milk and crackers. After Bill and the doctor left, Shannon came back into my room and plopped herself on the bed.

We were alone talking about the heart transplant and I said, "Shannon, what do you think about all this?"

She replied, "Mom, it is going to be hard either way."

I thought that was very astute for a sixteen year old and I have never forgotten it. Still, as a mother, I hurt for her also as I was sure it would color her life in a way unknown to both of us. There was nothing more I could offer her as I knew she had unexpected information to sort out in her mind. I hated to let her leave my hospital room with such a load on her shoulders but I knew I had to let her go on her way.

Mom's Diary, April 26, 1989: We had just started to eat dinner when David called with a report from Bill. David had arranged with Bill to make all of the calls to him, and he in turn, would relay all messages regarding Nancy to us. This seemed the best solution and they felt it would save time and save Bill from having to repeat information to all of us. Today's call was the worst yet. Nancy's heart is deteriorating and is pumping only 20 percent of the needed blood. The doctors cannot seem to stabilize her. She is not responding. There is some talk of a heart transplant. I was so shocked I could hardly believe what I was hearing. The thought of something so drastic had never crossed my mind. I did not know what to think. To make matters worse, Ed and Rosemary [my uncle and aunt] are visiting and we definitely do not want to spoil their visit. I think the Lord knows I needed a distraction just now to preserve my sanity. Ed is one of the Shank family's favorite visitors so when he left Los Angeles to visit us, the whole family clan made it a point to have a real party in his honor. So it was. We were all so busy that I scarcely had any free time. When our company left, I read everything I could find about heart transplants of which I knew nothing. It helped me understand Nancy's condition —not encouraging. I am agonizing over this but I have to keep ahold on my fears and emotions. Bill will call David if there is any change.

The instructions to the medical staff were, ". . . to let information sink in regarding a heart transplant, help patient work through 'shock' of being a candidate, encourage questions and concerns. Her family may need emotional support."

Chapter Ten

Will I Ever Wake Up from This Nightmare?

*S*o much bad news was coming my way that I was almost numb. Things were definitely going from bad to worse. I wasn't afraid then and accepted the facts in a fairly unemotional state. You've heard the comment, "I feel like I've been hit by a truck." Now I knew firsthand what that meant. If you think about it, perhaps

95

you can realize how I was feeling. First, I was taken by such surprise that I was stunned. And then I was in a state of shock because just a short time before I was merrily going along, still in control, when abruptly my life changed. The transformation was so drastic that I was enveloped by a feeling of complete helplessness, and nothing I could do would alter one thing.

It was noted on my chart that I was, "Alert, cooperative, anxious." The uncertainty of not knowing what was going to happen next made me very anxious. This was getting to be like a scene from a heavy drama and I was overwhelmed by the grayness and impending doom of the set.

Suddenly things started sinking in. After some time and soul searching, I did agree to think about having a heart transplant but I was not ready to decide to do it. In fact, I was leaning more against it than for it. I mentally listed all the pros and cons. The list of cons was very long, definitely longer than the pros.

First, there was no guarantee that I would live through the surgery and there were all the risks that accompany a major heart operation. If all went well, I would have to take a great deal of medicine for the rest of my life and have a routine of regular check-ups that included many tests. I would also have to keep daily charts of my blood pressure, temperature, and weight. My immune system would be selectively depressed so I would be susceptible to infection and probably have difficulty recovering from illness. The amount of information I got about what I would experience, the follow-up care, test after test after test, medications and possible side effects (That is how I got in this predicament in the first place!) was overpowering.

One of my favorite doctors, Dr. De Marco, a cardiologist (I never thought I would have a cardiologist until I was about eighty!), worked with Dr. Chatterjee. I could tell she was very intelligent and she was very pretty; when she smiled, she reminded me of my daughter, Shannon. Both she and Dr. Chatterjee were so devoted to the new heart transplant program that it seemed they were always at the hospital. I do not know how they kept up the pace for they would even pop in to see me evenings and on weekends. Dr. De Marco was my first female doctor, and it really has turned into a special relationship. We have become friends. One day she was talking with me about the proposed transplant and going over some details. Cyclosporine is a potent drug used to prevent transplant rejection and she mentioned, "One of the possible side effects of Cyclosporine is acne."

I was sitting there with one breast, bald, they wanted to cut out my heart, and she was telling me I may get acne! I had battled that when I was younger and I knew for sure I never wanted to see another blemish on my face, no matter what. I said to her, "What do you do about that?"

"We prescribe benzoyl peroxide and it usually goes away."

Immediately, I put "acne" on my "con list." Everything I was hearing was beyond my comprehension. I felt it really wasn't worth the effort and later made a mental picture of my new life. I compared it with my past, in which I figured I was in some kind of control. Was it worth even considering all of this?

Living longer and being with my family were two of the few items on my "pro list." But I did not want to be a burden and I didn't want my family to have to go through all of this. I tried to imagine if I would be anything like my old self. Living was my choice if I could have a reasonably normal lifestyle but there was risk and my luck was not running in a positive direction. No one could tell me and there were no guarantees. There were many, "What ifs?" Items kept popping up on the "con list." In my feeble thinking process, the "con list" loomed larger than the "pro list" probably because it was new and unknown.

After speaking with me at length, Dr. De Marco agreed to present my case to the transplant team for evaluation. I had "severe irreversible heart failure" and she thought that I had the support structure for transplantation, both factors that would qualify me for a new heart.

Dr. Magilligan stopped by my room frequently to see how I was and to answer questions. I am sure I asked the same ones repeatedly but he was patient. The medical staff helped me work through the shock of being a transplant candidate and offered emotional support as I received and integrated a great deal of information in a short period. I tried to keep my attitude positive but the odds against it were piling up.

Mom's Diary, April 27, 1989: I did not sleep well. Mentally, I asked myself how can I tell my first daughter goodbye? Lying in bed I watched the scenes go by ——first her babyhood, her growing-up years and then her completed college career. She had cheerfully packed away her favorite sorority souvenirs, her college textbooks, etc. as she detailed to her dad her new career plans. Moving to California was like moving to the moon to me, but I knew I must not stand in her way. The memories were like a movie that was quickly turning into a nightmare. Wearily, I got up and started the day as cheerfully as I could, not letting myself think of life without her.

Bill and I discussed often whether I should have a transplant. We were trying to keep this option confidential until a decision had been made one way or another. It was very difficult. A heart transplant was somewhat sensational and we did not want to worry our concerned family and friends any more than necessary. It had to be my decision but this one day, I asked Bill if he thought I should agree to a transplant and he replied, "Yes." That remark went on my "pro list" and weighed very heavily in my final decision for in my mind he was saying that he wanted me to live. I didn't think he would say "No," but we both knew the risks. If it did not go well, it could be a huge emotional and financial burden on the family. I did not want that.

Dr. Tulsky suggested that while I was thinking about the transplant, I should start the testing process to see if I would qualify. Just in case I decided to follow through, some time would be saved. I reluctantly agreed and a technician took five tubes of blood immediately. The qualifying process is extensive including numerous physical tests and interviews with almost everyone on the transplant team. This team consists of surgeons, cardiologists, transplant coordinators, exercise physiologists, a social worker, a psychiatrist, a pharmacist, a financial counselor, and any other person who might be pertinent to the case. In addition to severe heart disease, a strong support system, a good mental attitude, and a willingness to cooperate with follow-up care are essential ingredients in the qualifying process.

Two dentists from the dental school came to check my teeth since I was unable to go to them. A visit from a psychiatrist was offered but I declined, believing that I had plenty of people to talk with. There were so many people in and out of my room and I openly responded to their questions. Talking about my illness, my family, and the treatment plan was therapeutic.

I had almost daily visits from the social worker, Lily, while she was getting to know me and assess my family situation. It was her job to report whether I had the support I needed to get through all that was ahead. Entered in my file were the following notations:

Family Coping
Husband—quite supportive, keeps everything inside
Daughter—very competent, energetic, seems to be
   Dad's helper
Son—spent time just visiting with Mom, seemed
   comfortable
Nancy—has felt weak, thought she would feel better
   by now.

She always inquired about Shannon and Brendan and was interested in how they were coping with all that was happening to our family. She and I talked about clothes, food, and restaurants. We had several common interests and I enjoyed her visits. They gave me a connection with the outside world.

Mom's Diary, April 28, 1989: I am tired tonight. I expected some news on Nancy today but nothing arrived either by phone or letter. Marge [my mother-in-law] has been sending me letters which help because I worry about how Shannon and Brendan are coping with all of this. She is helping with the children and is helping run the household. What a great help she is in this time of great need. I try to keep busy all of the time. I did start a letter to Nancy but I gave it up after a few tries. I'll work on it in the morning when I can be more cheerful and offer her some encouragement. I know she is anxiously waiting and praying for a new heart. I'm sure all of our close friends are remembering her also. I am continuing to remind the Lord how much she is needed here in our family—and I feel I am asking for a miracle. I just keep saying, "Please give Nancy back to us if it is Your will." I do not know any other way. I do trust in God's goodness, but I feel He won't mind if I keep asking.

Waiting for test results was the most stressful thing during this period. On most days, I was scooted onto a gurney in the morning and then again in the afternoon. I think I visited every department in the medical center except obstetrics.

"I have become an expert on ceilings," I joked with those who came to push me around. One of the most worrisome tests for me was the bone scan which had to be done to make sure that the cancer had not spread. If I had cancer, it would eliminate me from being a heart transplant candidate. I started to consider that as a possibility and realized that my current problem would be over; there would be no decision to be made. There is nothing to a bone scan other than lying on a table so that part was easy. When the technician finished, she requested, "Would you please hold tight on the table for a minute? I need to have the radiologist take a quick look at the scan to make sure we have what we need."

She returned in a few minutes, "The doctor needs a few more pictures."

Alarmed, I said, "What did he find?"

"I don't know, he just said he needs another short scan."

I didn't believe her; I thought for sure she knew the reason. You can imagine what I thought. I was certain that the radiologist had spotted a tumor. I had to wait twenty-four hours for the results and my worries grew more harried every minute. Finally, I didn't care about my heart or anything else. I just didn't want to hear I still had cancer because coping with that would have put me over the edge. The next afternoon when Dr. De Marco came in, the first thing I asked her was, "What about the bone scan?"

"Oh, it was clear. There was one little hot spot but it was probably caused by one of the medicines."

I explained, "I could hardy sleep last night, I was so worried. When I was asked to remain for additional pictures yesterday, I was sure the cancer had returned."

"No," she said, "We feel certain you do not have cancer."

Picture extreme relief; my spirits soared and I began to feel normal again. No cancer! At last I was free of that worry. What a break. Sarcastically, I reasoned, "The darn chemotherapy practically killed everything else in my body, it certainly must have gotten any remaining cancer cells in the process."

Generally, the medical staff read my daily chart before they came into my room. Sometimes I could hear someone flipping through the pages outside my door. The thick file must have been getting more and more like a soap opera. "4-27-89: Patient has received and integrated a great deal of information in three days— attitude positive. She and husband have not decided."

Finally, I indicated I wanted to go home to think about the transplant and everything else that was going on. I wasn't ready to make the decision; I guess it just was too much to sort through and I needed some thoughtful reflection. It all happened so relatively fast, in a matter of months. I was to be gradually weaned from the CCU and the IVs and moved to the "floor" to adjust; then I could go home. The process was to take two weeks and I knew I could manage.

Chapter Eleven

Wake Up, Nancy!

*I*t was so nice to be unhooked from the IVs and the monitors, and to be moved into a regular hospital room. The staff in the CCU saw me off and wished me well. Celia wheeled me with all my belongings to my new room. It felt great; I didn't have any of those cords hanging from me and I was on my way to getting adjusted and going home. After spending all those weeks in intensive care where I was in bed or in a chair, now I had a bathroom, a desk, a mirror, a comfortable chair, a telephone, and room for guests. In an upbeat mood, I felt like I had moved to the Fairmont Hotel.

Organizing my room was first on the priority list. Moving very slowly, I arranged a few things on the desk and put my book on the bed tray. Then, I sat in the green, plastic upholstered chair to read the *San Francisco Chronicle*. I was so exhausted that it surprised me. I thought my strength would return immediately and I would begin to feel normal, and pick up my old life. Still, I must have had this deep lingering belief this was a monumental mistake and that it would go away when I left the CCU. Denial? Definitely! A sense of dejection started sinking my spirits.

Throughout the night, I had coughing spells that were difficult to control. I sat on the edge of my bed and the nurse checked me several times, each time saying, "Your vital signs are okay, so I don't know what could be causing the coughing."

"How encouraging," I thought mentally, "I'm on my way home." Again, the yo-yo rising up the string.

Dr. Chatterjee is a man of few words, but he inspires great confidence. He has a sense of peace and serenity about him and he always seems to be listening and observing intently. I imagine he would have a calming influence on any situation. The next morning, when he came in to see me, I told him about the coughing. Just then, Celia arrived to check on me and asked how I was making out in my new room. I was touched by her concern because I wasn't her patient anymore but her actions told me that she cared. Dr. Chatterjee put his hand on my heart and looked at the side of my neck and said, "You are going back to CCU." He turned to Celia and asked, "Is there a bed available?"

"Yes," she replied.

I did not have the opportunity to object and I think I was relieved. And so we reversed the procedure from the day before. Celia helped me get in the wheelchair and back we went to the CCU. My bed had already been given to someone else so I had a new room assignment. Now another fact shook me—I was going backwards. It just could't be.

In the eighteen hours I had been out of the CCU, I decided I did not want to live such a debilitated life and that I would have to agree to a heart transplant. Without a transplant, I would never have left the hospital and would not have lived much longer. Although I hadn't said anything to Bill yet, when Dr. Magilligan came in to see me, I told him, "I've decided you can put my name on the transplant list. I just can't live a life without a new heart."

To my amazement, he replied, "I already have; you are right at the top of the heart transplant list."

Anne, one of my nurses said, "All the nurses are praying you get a heart." And later, she said Celia told her, "She needs one soon."

There are surely some minor differences in how the transplant waiting lists work. To explain generally, after qualifying for a heart transplant, the sickest people, those not able to leave the hospital, get priority. There is not a separate list for every hospital participating in the program. The waiting list is a compilation of all the patients needing an organ and is administered by a separate regional organization.

The average wait for a heart to become available was three to six months. The idea of spending that much time in the hospital made me cringe. I said to myself, "I don't think I can stand waiting in this hospital room for that long. How can I cope with anything more? How can I possibly spend months just waiting anywhere?" I knew that was going to be a challenge but I had hope—and not much choice.

To my amazement, within one day, Dr. Magilligan came in and said, "We have a heart for you." Besides tissue match and blood type, a transplanted heart has to fit the patient, so similar body size is important. He went on, "This heart is from a man who is six feet tall and weighs about 135 pounds." Although, I wasn't that large, I did fall within the size range. "It is a plus, too, that he is in a close-by hospital so we can retrieve it and transplant it in a shorter period."

Suddenly, it was like a movie scene; excitement permeated the place. There was quite a flurry around my room. I didn't have a phone so a doctor stretched the cord from the nurses' station outside my room to my bed. I called my family to tell them what was happening and asked Bill if he thought I should take the heart that was being offered. He was shocked speechless to hear that there was a heart available so soon and for a few seconds was unable to say, "Go for it." I was still a little uncertain and it was as if I didn't want to make the decision alone.

I asked myself, "Do I really want to go through with this?" But now, I felt I was on a roller coaster and couldn't get off. There were so many people involved who were assuming I was going to have the operation. Word spread quickly that there was a heart for me and before I knew it, I had a full-blown cheering section. I did not have the courage to change my mind. Bill, Shannon, and Brendan left home and rushed to the hospital so they could wish me well before I went into surgery.

Shortly thereafter, before my family arrived, someone came into my room and said a mistake had been made. Someone at the Medical Center thought that 135 pounds was a very light weight for a six-foot man and called the hospital where he was located to request that he be weighed again. Sure enough, he was larger than I, so I was not a candidate for his heart. What a letdown! Relief, grief, fear, all melted into a blur, I said to myself again, "What next?" The elevator hit the basement floor again. I asked that they not tell me about a new heart unless they were absolutely sure it was for me. I didn't think I could cope much longer with the ups and downs. There were still a few people in my room when my family arrived. I had to tell them that it was a false alarm. It seemed as if no one knew quite what to say; everyone was disappointed. Bill, the children, and I had a short visit; they left dejected and I went back to reading my book—and the wait. It was Saturday, April 29, 1989.

One entry, by Dr. Magilligan, on my chart for April 30, 1989 was, "Feeling somewhat better—almost received a heart transplant last night and will readily, eagerly accept a heart when it becomes available." I am not sure how eager I was. Nevertheless, I was agreeable and moving forward.

In my room, there was a daily calendar on the wall under a big clock. Every morning, my nurse would come in and rip off the top page, exposing the new day. This was not an exciting life. I had no telephone calls, no flowers or company—other than immediate family members—to brighten my day. I looked at that calendar and couldn't imagine how long I would have to wait for my heart.

There was a possibility that a heart would never become available for me, but I wasn't too worried about it. From all the statistics I heard, I thought my chances were pretty good because I was one of the people at the top of the list of those waiting for new hearts—the one and only advantage of being among the sickest! Because, at the time, most of the donated hearts came from teenagers who had been in motorcycle or bicycle accidents, I was hopeful because my size range is similar to that of most teens. And I felt sad, thinking of a young person losing his or her life.

The next afternoon, there was quite a flurry outside my room. I could see my cardiologist, Dr. De Marco, sitting at the nurses' station. I saw doctors talking to each other, coming and going and talking on the telephone, but I did not think much about it. For some reason, it never dawned on me that the commotion had something to do with me. After a long while, Dr. Kwasman, who had been visiting me daily, came into my room and said, "We have another heart for you. It is from an eighteen-year-old boy and will have to be picked up in another city."

My immediate reply was, "Are you sure this time?"

"Everything looks good with this one."

"Do I have to decide this minute? How much time do I have to think about it?"

"Ten minutes!" I looked at the clock on the wall; the second hand seemed to be flying and I could not stop it.

The transplant team made sure everything was in order before they told me.

Again, they stretched the telephone receiver to my bed and I called my home to tell my family the good news. The doctor was dialing the number from the nurses' station. Wouldn't you know it, the line was busy, dial again, still busy. The minutes were going, dial again, still busy. Exasperation! With two teenagers, I pictured the phone being in use all evening. Because I am a former Bell Telephone employee, I knew that we could call the operator in case of an emergency and ask her to break in on the conversation. And so the doctor dialed "0" and made our request. She put him on hold for several seconds and reported that there wasn't anyone talking. "Darn, the phone must be off the hook or out of order," I commented. In panic, I suggested we telephone my neighbor, Jack, and ask him to go over and let my family know that I was trying to reach them. To my amazement, my addled brain could remember his telephone number and Dr. Kwasman quickly dialed it. Jack was the best neighbor. He was concerned about me and the family and he knew something was going on when he got the phone call from me. He went over to our house right away, and it was discovered the phone was off the hook. Jack was on pins and needles until he and his wife, Mel, got a full report. They continued to give us tremendous moral support.

All worked out and when my family arrived to see me, the preparations for my departure to the operating room were well underway so they did not stay long. I knew they were very worried and I did not want them to stay around the hospital for the many hours it would take to do the operation. They agreed and I gave each one a hug and a kiss and told them that I loved them. I couldn't bring myself to say, "This may be good-bye." I wanted them to walk out of the hospital full of hope. Also, at that moment, I did not have the emotional stamina to deal with all the tears that I knew would come flooding out. After Bill returned home and the children were settled in bed, he returned to the hospital to await word from Dr. Magilligan.

Mom's Diary, May 1, 1989: Morning brought the news from David that Nancy has a new heart. God answered our prayers. I was so jubilant that I could hardly put the phone down. But I had to gather my thoughts to call the girls to tell them that she had the operation Sunday night. The doctors did not want her to deteriorate any further so we are all thrilled. She would have gone downhill rapidly and they had a heart available. I guess relief came first, then joy. Thank you, God. Technically, the operation was a success. We now have to wait and see if she will reject or tolerate it. There is nothing more anyone can do; the main thing is for her heart to pump the blood on its own. We will wait and see. We are all completely wiped out.

Amazingly, I was not nervous about the surgery. I had time to think about it. In some countries, the operating room is called the "theater" so I figured that I would be the "star" and have everyone's attention while I was there. Also, I had all the information I could possibly consume about the procedure, and knew more than I ever wanted to know about hearts. I knew I wasn't going to feel anything and had mentally prepared myself for discomfort when I awakened. But by then, I thought I would be home free and the pain would be temporary and gradually disappear.

The operating room scene was completely different from what I had pictured. Operating rooms always looked so cold, scary and sterile. Whenever I looked at one, my imagination thought of something terrible going on inside. But, when people get in there, the whole place comes alive and takes on a new personality. It truly was a warm and friendly place. There were many people making all sorts of preparations and they all were trying to calm my fears. I was definitely the center of attention which was comforting. I heard the attending surgeon, Dr. Hanley call out, "We need to hurry because the heart is going to walk through the door at 6:05." I faded into oblivion.

After being on pins and needles for several hours, my sister, Anita called the medical center to ask if there was any news on how the operation was proceeding. She couldn't stand waiting any longer so she anxiously called the CCU. She heard cheering and clapping in the background. Word had just come that my new heart was beating on its own.

For some reason, still not completely clear, I did not awaken for three days from the anesthesia after the surgery. I was taken from the operating room to the ICU (intensive care unit) where I was classified as "relatively stable." The next day, Monday, noted on my chart was, "Of concern—mental status—not awake—not following commands." Tuesday, the ICU attending physician wrote, "Of major concern is her mental status. She opens her eyes but she doesn't move to deep pain and doesn't follow commands. The team is aware of this." Now, I consider it a little gift from God because I did not have any pain and slept through those first seventy-two hours of discomfort. It was much harder on those around me. My family and friends were very worried.

Dr. Chatterjee, Dr. De Marco, and Dr. Magilligan had worked long and hard on this new heart transplant program and I can only imagine how they were feeling. I was in the intensive care unit and there was much concern about my mental status because not only was I unconscious, I was not responding to stimulation of any kind.

Mom's Diary, May 2, 1989: I received a letter from Nancy today; she started it on April 22 and Bill mailed it for her. She doesn't complain and she tries to be cheerful. Late today, reality reared its ugly head and worry surfaced again. David called me with the latest report on Nancy. She is still not out of the anesthetic. They did a brain scan; her brain is functioning and her heart is pumping on its own. They aren't sure but think that she may have a sluggish liver. It will be seventy-two hours before we know anything. I am praying constantly and I am running out of words. Nevertheless, I do have peace of mind that all of us are doing our best and I know God will then take over for us. We will accept His decision——life or death——there is no other way.

Although unconscious, I recollect about three or four things that happened around me. One, a man was ordering me to open my eyes, which I did for a split second and had a glimpse of people standing around my bed. I heard someone say, "I've never seen anything like this." I can also remember trying to listen for Bill's voice but to no avail. He said he was there and he did talk to me. I remember what I thought was a small rake being rubbed on the bottom of my feet and the palm of a hand coming down on my face stopping just before it hit my nose. Later, Dr. De Marco told me the neurologists probably were trying to get a reaction from me. Finally, I remember masses of black and white, interchanging as if they were fighting each other. The black seemed to me to be death and the white life. I felt I could choose which I wanted. It was a struggle, for the masses kept changing sizes. The white shapes started getting larger than the black ones, I was fighting to have the white overtake the black. And then, I finally awakened.

Celia was standing by my bedside as my eyes blinked open. When I saw her, I knew I was alive. She had come over from the CCU to see how I was doing. She never forgot me and went out of her way to see if there was any change in my condition. Immediately, a neurologist was at my bedside asking me questions like, "What year is this?" "Who is the mayor of San Francisco?" and "How old are you?" I'm sure he was checking to see if I had brain damage. I was proud that I could answer these questions, especially the one about the mayor of San Francisco, because I lived in Oakland. I knew my brain was working and I was functioning on my own. The doctor wrote in the log, "Happily, Mrs. Pedder awakened. She is alert and oriented. We extubated her and she is doing very well." At least it was a beginning.

Mom's Diary, May 3, 1989: When I get up in the morning, my thoughts fly right to Nancy and the

♡

question is still there —— What will this day bring?
When Bill called, we heard, "Nancy is conscious."
Thank God, I whisper as I await the next sentence.
"Her metabolism is slow and her liver is sluggish."
But she is still alive, I reason and hope springs right
up. She is in an oxygen mask and Bill was not
permitted to stay very long. Her vital signs are good
and the doctors say her progress is normal for her
condition. We passed on this glorious message and I
could hear all of the tears and shouting over the
telephone. Anita Marie is completely overcome with
emotion as they are very close. I try hard to put
aside all of my unanswered questions and am leaving
Nancy in God's hands.

The moral support and friendship I received from the medical staff were superb. I had been living in the hospital for six long weeks; they had become like family. The heart transplant program at UCSF was new; I was the third recipient and the first woman. They were all pulling for me. Mary, my nurse from the CCU of whom I'd become very fond told me that while she was at home, she and her little boy, Michael, would scream, "Wake up, Nancy!"

"And wake up I did, Michael!"

Chapter Twelve

A New Beginning

Mom's Diary,
May 4, 1989: For the first
time in months, I awakened
and heard a bird outside my
window. It was the first
time in a while that I sang
along a cheerful reply to his
song. Somewhere in the back
of my mind, I remembered
that bluebirds bring good
luck. I let my mind wander,

and I saw signs of spring which now I could at least enjoy. Spring seems to have a special meaning to me. The telephone ended my thoughts. David called to report that the nurses had gotten Nancy up for three hours to avoid pneumonia. They have taken her off the oxygen. This is the first good news all week. She will need a good biopsy before she can leave the hospital and they have scheduled it for Friday. The doctor told Bill that she would have died without a new heart. All of this pointed out to me that God gave Nancy back to us and certainly He will give her whatever she needs to pull through all of this.

Recovery from the heart transplant in my case was not exactly routine. I was weak from being in bed for so many weeks and had very limited use of my right arm because of a previous procedure. I could not even get out of a chair without some help.

The first night out of intensive care was an ordeal for all concerned. The nurses who were to take care of the transplant patients had special training. I could tell my night nurse was nervous but we were getting along fine. She helped me to a chair, told me she had to get some medications and would be back in a few minutes. She showed me two buttons to push if I needed her; one was red and one was blue. I was beginning to feel very tired and wanted to get back in bed. I waited and waited and she didn't return. This was a different experience from the CCU, where all I had to do was blink and someone was instantly in my room. After watching the clock for twenty minutes, I decided that I'd push the button in five minutes if she didn't return. And then I added another five. Thirty minutes was the absolute longest I was going to sit there. I was getting anxious and I was sure that wasn't good for me. Now, I had to decide which button to push. I reasoned back and forth, "The red is probably for help. The blue is probably for the code blue team—but maybe it is the other way around." Finally, I pushed the red one and I could hear an alarm start screeching down the hall. Suddenly, three nurses charged into the room in a panic. Immediately, I knew that I had pushed the wrong button. One quickly ran over and turned off the light that triggered the alarm. They were visibly relieved to see that I was okay. My nurse sheepishly said, "I'm sorry, I forgot you." The whole scene was like a comedy movie; it was so funny but I did not dare laugh.

One day, everyone was excited because Carlos, the number-one heart transplant patient, had climbed one flight of stairs. Now, I knew why; it would be like climbing a mountain for the average person. Climbing a flight of stairs seemed like a long way off for me. I couldn't imagine how I would do it but hearing of his accomplishment made me optimistic.

When I was moved to a regular hospital room, education began on all of the different aspects of my new life. There were the medications that I would have to administer myself. The pharmacist spent time going over all of them with me, telling me what each was for and the potential side effects. The physical therapist, Chris, came every day to "work out" with me. She was very supportive and kept me motivated. That was one of the highlights of the day because I could leave my room and see what was going on in the hall. I felt like I was being eased back into the real world. Numerous doctors, nurses, and medical students followed my progress. I looked in the mirror for only the second time in six weeks and discovered that my hair was really coming back. Happy day! Jokingly, I would ask my nurses if there were any gray in it. The general response was, "It looks like a little." It took about two years, but my hair did grow back curlier and fuller than before and amazingly the gray has all disappeared.

Mom's Diary, May 8, 1989: I received a letter from Marge [my mother-in-law] today from which I gained much information. A woman's point of view is a big help to us right now. Nancy is making some progress. Just now she is getting settled into a room. She is so weak that her progress requires much effort on her part. Marge is assisting on the home front especially with helping the children cope with school work and deal with their mother's changes. Bill is home in the evenings. It was so good of Marge to share these details with us. I called my girls as I'm sure all enjoyed and appreciated this response. I can see from this letter that Nancy is going to have a very difficult time just regaining her strength. She will need much more support to get her through this ordeal. Our job is to figure out how our family can get the most support to her. We need some good old Indiana-brand encouragement delivered to her very soon.

There was a physician, Dr. Molnar, in the hospital who visited me often. He received a new heart the year before at another facility and worked in the pathology department at UCSF. He was following my case and he stopped by one day and to my great surprise asked, "Do you want to see your first heart?" With some hesitation, I said, "Yes, but I want my husband to be with me because I'm not sure how I will react." In the back of my mind, I was thinking that maybe I really hadn't needed a new heart—not that it would make any difference at this point, but I wanted to see for myself. Then, Dr. Molnar told me what to expect. He said, "Your heart will look perfectly normal in size because it hasn't been diseased long enough to be enlarged."

I thought for a minute to let that fact sink in. Then I asked, "Really?"

"Sometimes, they are as large as basketballs."

"You're kidding!"

"No . . . Your heart was in very good condition with no plugs and little fat on the outside. Most people your age have a layer of fat around their hearts but yours had very little. It probably would have served you well for your lifetime."

"You mean that if I had not had the chemotherapy drug, my first heart would still be functioning well?"

"That's correct."

I got permission to leave the tenth floor and Bill wheeled me to the pathology department. Dr. Molnar was waiting at the door and we could tell he was excited about our visit. I was a little apprehensive because I had only seen labs like this in the movies. I was looking all around trying to see what was in there. There were long tables with microscopes setting on them. Dr. Molnar walked right over to what looked to me like a huge ice chest. He opened it and got my heart out. I was trying to hold my breath, a trick I learned when I was a child if I didn't want to taste or smell something. I didn't want to smell the formaldehyde. My former heart was gray and looked exactly like all the pictures you see in books. To my surprise, I looked at it in a very detached way with no emotion. I asked, "How long do you keep these?"

"Not very long. There really is no need to keep them after a certain point."

I was a little disappointed but I didn't say anything. How could they not keep my heart and use it for research or something? He then guided us to another section of the room saying, "Come on over here; I have set up some slides for you to look at. I want to show you some samples of your heart and some samples of a healthy heart so you can see exactly what cardiomyopathy looks like under the microscope."

"Oh, okay," I responded, but I really didn't want to do that. We looked at slides with samples of a healthy heart and compared them to slides of samples taken from mine. The walls of my heart had thickened and become like a rubber band that wouldn't contract and expand. We could see a difference in the connective tissue between the strands in the muscle. There was much more space between mine. Definitely, I needed a new heart. My mind was at peace now on that score. We thanked Dr. Molnar, left the pathology lab and Bill wheeled me back to my room. I was in an upbeat mood after seeing my heart and thinking about going home.

Mom's Diary, May 9, 1989: Today I am eighty years old. Never did I ever think I'd live this long. Peg and Pete called to wish me a Happy Birthday as did Anita Marie and Monica. The biggest and best present was Nancy's call. I felt as if 1,000 pounds had been lifted off my heart. I am encouraged that she will be okay. Just to hear her voice and be assured she is doing okay was worth a million dollars.

I was still being monitored around the clock but soon there was talk about going home. I was looking forward to continuing my recovery, regaining my strength, and beginning a regular life. If all went well, I could be released in time to spend Mother's Day at home. At this time, I was euphoric. My friend, Jennie, was going to bring dinner over and make me a mud pie for dessert to have for my homecoming. After seven weeks of hospital food, I couldn't wait to celebrate with a substantial piece of my favorite pie. My values got a little out of kilter at this time and I dreamed of the pie. It is a scrumptious dessert with an Oreo cookie crust, which is firm and crunchy, filled with cold, smooth ice cream and smothered with velvety, soft, thick chocolate fudge sauce. I knew it wouldn't be on my heart diet but I decided that I needed a treat.

JENNIE'S MUD PIE

Crust

18 Oreo or Hydrox chocolate cream sandwich cookies
1/3 cup melted butter
Crush cookies to fine crumbs. Add melted butter. Mix well.
Press around sides and bottom of nine inch pie pan. Chill.

Filling

1 quart coffee ice cream
2 squares unsweetened chocolate
1/2 cup sugar
1 tablespoon butter
1 (5 1/2 to 6 oz.) small can evaporated milk

Fill pie shell with coffee ice cream. Freeze. Melt chocolate over hot water and stir in sugar and butter. Slowly add evaporated milk. Cook over hot water until thickened. Chill. Spread chocolate mixture over top of ice cream. Freeze.

I had spent time thinking about what it was going to be like when I did return home and how I would deal with what was awaiting me. I knew life at home had changed since I went in the hospital seven weeks before. From the signals I had picked up, indeed, there had been a change and it naturally did not include me. It was a gradual process that probably was a coping mechanism for my family. Life went on without me and by the end of the ordeal having no mom at home was the norm. Remembering growing up the oldest in a large family helped me sort out what family life was all about. I knew that I shouldn't get upset and that I needed a good sense of humor. I had to expect that I would be an outsider for a period. It really did not hurt my feelings at all. In fact, I had to chuckle to myself at some of the proposals I was getting when one of my children would say something like, "You know, Mom, I've become very independent while you have been in the hospital. I don't think I'm going to need you to tell me what to do when you get home." I had plenty of time to think about how I was going to respond when I did go home.

Now, I had a telephone in my room so I had access to the outside world. One of the first phone calls I made was to my friend, Carol. Her husband, Bill, answered the phone and I'll never forget how genuinely happy he was to hear from me. When I announced who was calling he said, "Nancy, really? I don't believe it. This is *wonderful!*" He made my day.

The most dreaded thing for me at the time was that my body might reject my new heart even though I had been told rejection was common and usually could be controlled with medication adjustments. I felt certain it wouldn't happen to me; it just wouldn't seem fair after all I'd been through. The way it is determined if rejection is occurring is by doing a heart biopsy. Although not painful, it is a stressful experience for me. I just feel a "little pin prick" and the procedure usually takes under half an hour, and several more hours to get the results from the pathology department.

I was to have a biopsy and if there were no rejection, I could go home on Mother's Day. The first thing I thought of was the pie; I could taste it. I was not very strong but was walking laps in the corridor every day and starting to feel as if I would survive. So, in anticipation, I began sending my personal belongings home with Bill. He told our family and a few friends that I would be home in time for Mother's Day dinner. Jennie started making the mud pie. Things were definitely looking up.

And then came probably the lowest point for me in the whole adventure. I don't know what it was, perhaps a foreboding or a sixth sense, but I could always tell when someone walked in my room to tell me something I didn't want to hear. It was Saturday morning, May 13, the day before Mother's Day, almost two weeks since my operation. My new heart sank even before Dr. De Marco could say, "You have some rejection and you can't go home yet. We'll do another biopsy in a few days and see if the rejection is under control." I was back on the roller coaster and I felt like I was sinking in muddy water. The highs and lows had finally gotten to be too much. I was certain that I could not get up after being batted down once again. My whole world slid out from under me; I just didn't think I could cope with any more bad news.

My nurses could tell that I was extremely disappointed. They left me alone for a few hours and kept everyone out of my room. It was the weekend and there wasn't much going on so they put a sign on my door saying, "Do Not Enter." They intercepted my breakfast and the lab technician who came to draw blood at the crack of dawn every day, so I could sleep in—quite a treat in a hospital. I tried to cry but I couldn't. In hindsight, I think it worked out for the best because I was very weak and being at home would have been a worry for everyone. Reality finally helped me accept that my recovery would be a slow process with many ups and downs. I came to terms with this disappointment.

Jennie had not heard the latest report and she brought dinner and the mud pie to our house on Mother's Day for the celebration of my homecoming. When Bill told me, I said, "My pie, darn! It will be gone by the time I get home." I knew everyone would be as enthusiastic about it as I was so I added, "Please save at least one piece." He agreed that he would try to guard the pie until I could leave the hospital.

Events that included my children were very important to me. I wanted desperately to be home in time to see Brendan's graduation from eighth grade and to be a part of the celebration. My surgeon, Dr. Magilligan, came by my room to say, "I personally guarantee that you will be at your son's graduation." Families were very special to him and he realized how important it was for me to be there. I smiled. He definitely made me the happiest person in the hospital that day.

Several days later, I was taken in a wheelchair to the cath lab for my next biopsy. The result was negative, no rejection; I was overjoyed. Now I could definitely plan on going home. The pie— I could see a huge piece on a plate with the shiny chocolate just waiting for a plunge from my fork!

Dr. Chatterjee is a very special person. One thing I learned was when he says you are going to be okay, you know you are going to be okay. The next day when he stopped by for one of his regular visits, I said, "Thank you for saving my life." He did not say a word. He simply lifted his hand, shook it back and forth and pointed upward. I knew exactly what he meant. He turned and quietly walked out the door.

Dr. De Marco also dropped into my room about 5:00 P.M. and asked, "Do you want to go home?"

"When can I go?" My spirits began to soar in anticipation.

"How about now?" she replied. I couldn't believe my ears.

Word spread or perhaps they knew about my departure beforehand but it seemed like all my new friends were stopping by to say goodbye. I was getting excited. Things were definitely looking up.

Dr. Magilligan came into my room to give me last-minute advice and several telephone and beeper numbers. He wanted me to call him or Dr. De Marco if I had any problems or worries. His parting remark was, "See, I told you I'd have you home in time for your son's graduation."

I responded, "Thank you, you did a great job!"

I called Bill, "Guess what? I can go home."

"When?"

"Dr. De Marco said that it will probably take a couple of hours to get me discharged because my nurse has to give me some instructions and I don't know what else."

"Okay, I'll leave here in about an hour."

"Bill, I hope my pie is still there."

"There was one piece in the freezer when I left this morning."

"Great, I'll see you soon."

My dinner tray arrived and I said to the man who delivered it, "No thank you, I'm having dinner at home and mud pie for dessert." He didn't even smile; he simply took the tray and walked out the door.

Bill left work early and came over to the medical center and right up to my room. There was a hustle-bustle of activity and I was excited. Dr. De Marco was in and out giving me last-minute instructions and the phone numbers to call for any questions or problems. My nurse was helping me get my things packed up. Bill went to get the car and my nurse went to get a wheelchair. I protested, "I don't need that. Why do I have to get in the wheelchair? I've been walking laps in the hall for two weeks."

"It is the rule of the hospital. You have to stay in the chair until you get outside the door," she replied. She helped me get situated, piled my belongings including a pillow on my lap and escorted me downstairs to the front door. She assisted me into the car and suggested, "You may want to put the pillow on your chest if the seat belt hurts you." Like any incision, it was tender for a few weeks. It takes the sternum about three months to heal so after surgery I had to be somewhat protective of my chest. It is especially important to keep arm movements even. For example, I wouldn't raise only one arm over my head or lift something heavy with one arm. I would use two hands and keep myself balanced.

It was great to be out in the fresh air. I took deep breaths and was very aware of how wonderful it felt to be alive. It was nippy, windy, and the fog was wisping around the building and the cars, giving me a chill. I'd forgotten how it felt. People were coming and going, rushing out the sliding door, getting into cars and darting across the street. I was now part of all the movement and it was great, the new beginning of a normal life. Somewhat nervous, I thought about the possibility of a car accident on the way home. The last thing my chest needed was a bump; even with the pillow securely buckled under my seat belt, my imagination went wild. The ride over the Bay Bridge to Oakland was uneventful, thank goodness. I remembered my last trip across the bridge to San Francisco. It seemed so long ago. This was a much happier occasion.

Mom's Diary, May 23, 1989: David called me and began by saying, that Bill brought Nancy HOME! I gasped, "At last—happy day." David interrupted me to say that she has to go back to the hospital Friday as an outpatient for another biopsy. He couldn't wait to tell me she would be an outpatient and not have to stay at the hospital overnight. Well, nothing was going to spoil my happiness. It just curled all around me. I kept repeating out loud, "Nancy's home." She is in her own home. It is true. This is absolutely my best news and I held on to every minute of it. I called the girls and their relief matched mine. Joy was in the Shank households. Nancy will do so much better functioning in her own home. How I wish that I could send Carolyn to cook her meals for her. She is such a good cook especially when someone needs special food. The distance and time make that impossible right now. Believe me, we will sleep much better tonight. She was supposed to call me, but evidently she wasn't up to it as it is after 11:00 P.M. and she hasn't called. Anyway ── I'm happy she is at home.

I arrived home Tuesday evening, May 23, 1989, seventeen days before Brendan's graduation. Since my release from the hospital had not been specifically planned, the children didn't expect me. Shannon was gone to swimming practice and Brendan was on his way out to play basketball. He gave me a hug and was out the door.

"See ya later."

The camera on the real world started rolling again.

Bill opened the refrigerator and started to get out leftovers for dinner. Friends had been bringing in food for many weeks so there was plenty to choose from. I sat at the dining room table just looking around my house. Everything looked just the same, as if I hadn't been gone more than a few hours. It was a strange sensation, but I was elated to have my dinner on a table rather than a hospital tray. Bill served the food and waited on me. I ate, saving room for the mud pie. It was time; I got up from my chair, walked into the kitchen and opened the freezer door. I peered in and couldn't spot the pie.

"Where is the pie?" I called.

"It's in there; I saw it this morning."

"I can't find it. I'm probably looking right at it."

Bill came into the kitchen and poked around and said, "I don't see it; I can't imagine what happened to it. I know it was here."

Since it was made of ice cream, I knew it had to be in the freezer and no place else. "It has to be here; I'll just keep looking."

Slowly (I couldn't move too fast), I took everything out of the freezer and the lonely piece of mud pie was nowhere in sight. By the time I had returned the frozen food to its place, I had spent thirty minutes looking for my prized dessert. Cleaning out the freezer was not what I had in mind for my first night home. I walked over to the sink to throw away some ice cubes and my eyes immediately were drawn to a small saucer with a solitary fork on it sitting in the dish pan. It was pretty clean but had some traces of chocolate sauce on it. I picked it up and inspected it closer.

"My pie, it's gone!"

My disappointment immediately dissolved into laughter. This was typical family life. I was happy to be alive and in my own home. I know who ate the pie, but I'm not telling.

On the Friday evening before Brendan's graduation, there was a party for the eighth-graders and their parents. Betty and Dave invited us to dinner beforehand and we had a very special evening with them, Julie, another friend for many years, and our boys. It was my first outing in two months. Getting dressed up was a joy; it did wonders for my spirits and made me feel like I was on top of the world. It was glorious to focus on something other than my health.

Graduation day was very special in many ways. Aunt Rosemary and Uncle Ed came from Los Angeles to be with us and help with the party afterward. Anita and Peter, Mel and Jack and all the Pedders rallied around. In the graduation processional, the graduates each carried a rose which they presented to their parents as they walked up the aisle. As Brendan stepped out of line, he gave me his rose and a kiss. I'm told that there was not a dry eye in the place. I was so happy that I was alive to help him with the transition to high school. "Thank you, God." I said, for I realized He was with me through this day especially, and I was most grateful.

The first year after a heart transplant is full of adjustments. I was going to the medical center in San Francisco weekly, sometimes twice a week. I couldn't drive yet, so Bill would take me to the rapid transit station on his way to work. I would take the train or have someone take me all the way to the medical center. I felt as if I still lived at the hospital; the only difference was I didn't spend the night. It was a time when my body was getting used to its new heart so there were numerous biopsies to make sure that rejection was kept under control. Medicine changes were frequent; follow-up tests were numerous.

I was getting to be well-known in the cath lab where they did the biopsies. By this time, we were all friends and they were genuinely interested in my progress and always asked about my family. Curtis, a cardiovascular technologist was always there to greet me and help get me prepared. He is so friendly, has a good sense of humor and makes me feel at ease. Dr. Yock is an outstanding physician and having him there made me feel confident that all would go well. He is now working at Stanford, and Dr. Ports, another excellent cardiologist, has taken his place. He instills confidence and that helps me relax. Georgie, another assistant who is always full of fun and energy would say, "You again? You keep turning up like a bad penny." I'd laugh and say, "You're right, but not by choice." She kept my mind off the procedure by telling me about her winery, Magnolia Cellars, which she started. She is very talented and even painted the beautiful magnolia blossom that graces the bottle's label. Olga and Judy made me feel good by their special caring manner.

It was an ordeal for me at first because I had so little stamina. I expected I would wake up every morning and feel at least a tiny bit better and stronger, but it wasn't quite like that. It would take me a half-hour to get dressed. Putting on my pantyhose was a major project. It is hard to imagine being that weak unless you have experienced it. I would reach plateaus and after a few days, start the climb again. Often, it was discouraging, but somehow I managed to begin again until my strength returned. To my surprise, getting better was so much work; it took commitment and determination.

Mom's Diary, May 25, 1989: I talked with Nancy on the phone today. It was good to hear her voice. Just knowing she is still with us is a miracle. I tried not to express the shock I felt when told about her present situation. She is so weak everything is an effort for her, even getting out of bed. She is taking forty-four pills a day (and I gripe about six). I ask myself how in the world can she keep track of them? She now has frequent biopsies in San Francisco as an outpatient. As she tells me these things, I ask myself, "What kind of a life is this?" I cannot even imagine the effort it would take to do the simplest things. I find myself questioning, "Is this to be her future?" I realize I have no right to question God's plan for Nancy, but I would love Him to send in a second team to help right now. What a life for our Nancy, but she is alive, that is enough for now.

My appearance had changed and I did not look like my old self at all. Every time I looked in the mirror, my spirits sank because what I saw was a fat, bald person. I still had to wear the wig because my head just had fuzz on it and I was bloated from the cortisone I was taking. The fullness was especially noticeable in my face. I was self-conscious about my scar which ends at the top of my collar bone. As I would stare inside my closet, I would ask myself, "What am I going to wear to hide it?" Several times, casual acquaintances didn't even recognize me. I would say, "Hi" to someone in passing and get a blank look and have to refresh their memory with my name. Invariably they were embarrassed, so after several episodes I didn't speak to people unless they spoke first. It did not hurt my feelings, because I could see what the problems were by looking in the mirror. I had been told it was temporary which made me hopeful that I would eventually look like me again. I had to like myself before I could expect it of others so I tried to do my best and call on all of my resources, especially a sense of humor. I hope I succeeded. Repeatedly, I thought of people who have their looks permanently changed from accidents or burns. You know yourself that you are the same person inside but others treat you differently.

A self-image is important and I found myself thinking about the perception people have of others. Since my situation was temporary, I could keep it in perspective but I know it would be very difficult to adjust if it were permanent.

Chapter Thirteen

Pick Yourself Up, Dust Yourself Off, and Start All Over Again!

Mom's Diary,
June 2, 1989: Nancy
called me herself this
morning. I could kiss the
telephone for bringing me her

133

upbeat voice. She sounded so cheerful and it was contagious. I sensed she was trying to be her old self and she said that she is feeling better each day. It took a long time for her to tell me some of her greatest achievements so I could share in her struggles. She never emphasized the effort it took to get her life back, just the great results. I could just feel her relief jumping along the telephone and into my ear. This was a big day for me. She told me she is going up and down stairs and spends a lot of time organizing all her medications. Since I have not taken much medicine over the years, I can't even imagine what it is like for her. She said that she does get tired. I tried to tell her not to go into crowds. She told me that she had even been to a luncheon at her friend, Linda's, which makes me so happy. She loves her friends and this is so good for her to get out. In her growing-up years that was always her special treat so I knew that she was on her way back to normal. Her last biopsy was okay. Sweet music, believe me. I hated to have to end this conversation. Nevertheless, I sensed from her voice that she was getting tired so I suggested we stop talking so we would have something to tell each other the next time. Really, this was just *my day and here I am living to hear all about her trip back to life. I put the phone down and whispered, "Thank you, Lord," once more. What more could I ask? She is on the road to recovery.*

Finally home, I tried to get back to the routine chores around the house and even found pleasure in doing them. I had been so active before hitting rock bottom, not knowing if I'd ever even be able to sweep the floor again. I am a person who follows all of the doctor's orders so I knew I would do everything Dr. DeMarco told me to do. It was even more important now that I keep my part of the bargain, which was to follow faithfully the daily regime set up for me following the transplant. To this day, I am conscientiously fulfilling my promises in that regard. Chris, my physical therapist, told me to walk daily out of my house for six minutes, and then turn around and come home. Then each day or so, I was to add a few extra minutes to the routine. I was steadfast and did it first thing in the morning. Before long, I was walking for thirty minutes. Today, I walk, at a brisk pace, about two and a half miles a couple of times a week.

During my college years, I was a lifeguard and enjoyed outside water activities. Swimming has always been a wonderful sport for me for physical fitness and mental health so I really wanted to get back to it. There is something about immersing myself in the swimming pool that I love. It is therapeutic to put my head down and close out my surroundings. It provides a great time to think, ponder things, great and small or just let my mind wander. It is a splendid way to start the day and gives me a sense of accomplishment. My swimming friends, including Elise, Lynn, Bonnie, Susan, and Barbara are very special. I see Elise almost every morning. We have so much in common including our Midwestern roots and large families. We have fun and if she isn't there I worry about her. We chat as we swim a few laps; then I put my head down and get to work. Lynn and Barbara worry about me to this day if I'm absent. When Dr. De Marco gave me permission to return to the swimming pool, I started swimming my laps. I was slow at first but gradually built up my stamina. At the time of this writing, nine years later, I swim three quarters of a mile five days a week. Recently, Elise and I were discussing how important it is to commit to exercise. I am an example of how it can make a difference.

Mom's Diary, June 16, 1989: Nancy sent us a picture along with her letter. Just looking at it, reminds me again of her gift of life. We all think she looks good in spite of all the physical problems she has overcome these past months. My own conclusion is that God has something very special planned for her and so He gave her back her life to accomplish it. So, I intend to enjoy every minute of her life that I can. I become more aware every day of the great gift God gave our two families in returning her in health to all of us.

However, my body would get so tired in a way I had never before experienced. My mind would have lists of things I wanted to do daily, tasks that before I had done easily. I was so discouraged in the evening when I had accomplished only about one-third of them. My body would scream for the prone position. Stretching out on the bed would be such a relief. My body felt like it was part of the mattress as if it were soothing my tired muscles. After a nap or a night's sleep, I was refreshed and started again. That in itself told me I was making small gains daily. Even a little bit of progress was welcome and helped me on my way. I tried not to look back but I realized that not too long before, every little step was going in the wrong direction.

Life with my family had changed; fortunately it was temporary. Initially, when I returned home from the hospital, I was an outsider because life had gone without me. From my hospital bed, I had seen this coming so I was prepared. Gradually, I resumed my role without charging back in to take control. I really wanted to be the full-time mom again.

One thing that struck me at our first family dinner was how the table manners had deteriorated. A typical mom, I was appalled but I didn't say anything—then. The never-before chewed pencil and pen tops reminded me that the house had been boiling over in anxiety. Bill wanted me to take it easy and didn't want me to overdo but I was anxious to demonstrate that I was fine. Very few times in the past had I heard, "Don't do the dishes." Now I did them but it took me forever. No one knew for sure what to expect including me but I was determined to get family life back to normal. Shortly, everything was rolling along routinely.

One night when I had gone to bed around 9:00 P.M. and had just gotten myself settled with a book, Shannon came in and said, "Mom, will you do me a favor?"

I thought to myself that she probably wanted me to proofread an essay. I was trying to make every effort at being a "regular mom," however not looking forward to dragging my body out of bed, I still replied, "Sure, what do you want me to do?"

"Would you come and speak to my Bay Area Social Concerns Class?"

Rather surprised, I said, "Of course, I'd be happy to do that, but what would you want me to talk about? I'm not sure I have any credentials or enough knowledge to talk about Social Concerns."

"You could talk about your heart transplant."

"Well, I guess I could do that."

She was so pleased, "Good, I'll tell Mr. Kastel tomorrow and we can work out the details later."

The Bay Area Social Concerns class was a one-semester elective course for seniors at Bishop O'Dowd High School. It was initiated by Mr. Kastel to acquaint students with life in the real world. He brought speakers to the classroom from all walks of life. Many of Shannon's friends have commented that they learned more in that class than they did in many others.

This gave me the incentive I must have needed, another interest outside myself. I wanted to awaken my brain with intellectual pursuits which had been lying dormant for months. So I did make the effort.

Putting together a presentation on organ transplantation for the class of seniors was a stimulating task. Shannon joined me as part of the program the first time so she could give her perspective as a family member. We had decided that besides speaking about heart transplants, we would invite her classmates to mark the dot on their driver's license agreeing to become organ donors should the occasion arise. We also encouraged them to wear helmets if they rode bicycles or motorcycles since those accidents are where many donated hearts and other organs come from. We had no trouble holding the attention of our audience and were asked many interesting questions. Shannon graduated and went on to college but Mr. Kastel invited me back to speak to his classes every semester thereafter. Other opportunities to speak to groups became available and I was always amazed at the interest. Most people just do not know that much about the success of organ transplants. And that is how I got started on this writing project. It just seemed like a good next step.

My brother, David, commented recently, "A heart transplant is something you've heard of but know absolutely nothing about." Many people are curious about how it feels to have someone else's heart. It feels the same as my first one. I'm not aware of any difference; in fact, if I didn't have a scar, I wouldn't be conscious of it at all. I'm often asked about drug side effects. It would take two pages for me to list them but the possibilities range from nausea and dizziness to lymphoma. Another question I'm asked frequently is if I know the family that donated their son's heart to me and the answer is "No, I do not." Dr. DeMarco told me I had a lot to deal with and so did the family who had experienced the tragic loss of a loved one. The family was told that I was a young mother with two children and we all appreciated their donation. Some organ recipients meet their donors but, as a rule, it doesn't happen. Never ever did I dream I would feel as well as I did before I had cancer so I shouldn't be amazed when people are surprised to see me looking normal, energetic, and healthy.

After two years, I felt fine but as if I were about 98 percent of my old self. My friends were very supportive and little by little, my social life picked up. I was doing everything I did before I had the cancer, keeping up with my teenagers, enjoying family and my wonderful friends, doing volunteer work, etc. I was napping almost daily but I just couldn't seem to get to 100 percent. I was bloated from medication and my muscles desperately needed toning; I was not as strong as I was before my mastectomy. If I had to live that way, I could have accepted it. I really did not know what to expect when I began my recovery but I was so close now that I was determined to do something about getting back to the top.

A friend, Staige, told me about her experiences working in a weight training program. She encouraged me to talk to her trainer, Kriss and, after putting it off for months, I contacted her. She was so friendly and positive on the telephone and her enthusiasm transferred to me so I looked forward to meeting with her. When I arrived at her gym and opened the door, a steep flight of stairs came into view. Pausing for a second, I thought, "Oh no, can I do this?" I looked at them and started the climb; it was a chore to get to the top. This reinforced what I already knew; I was out of shape. I turned the corner at the top of the steps and there waiting for me was a beautiful, glamorous woman, Kriss. We had a very productive interview and I decided right then that this was the solution for me. She was very knowledgeable about the body which was reassuring for I did not want any injuries after all I had been through. She told me she was a little nervous at first working with me because she had no experience with a heart transplant client. In her very professional manner, she never let on that she was concerned.

Today, I work out with free weights and Nautilus equipment three times a week. I work out with Kriss once a week and she keeps me motivated with her motto, "We are Options women and we can do anything!" Kriss has become a special friend; she is a beautiful person inside and out. I can pinpoint my feeling 100 percent to when I started weight training with Kriss. Lifting weights is something I may not have done if I hadn't had a heart transplant; it is a challenge for me, in other words—hard work. Within a few months, my strength improved. Exercise definitely was the turning point.

As the months have progressed, I have become convinced that exercise is one of the most important things we can do for ourselves. It makes you feel good mentally and physically. Kriss and I discuss this frequently and agree that you have to give it priority and if you make it a habit, you do get results. When I am asked for tips on recovering from a catastrophic illness, I put exercise at the top of the list. I quickly add that you must consult with your physician. The benefits can be monumental. Even if you can only do something small, it is a beginning. After my heart transplant, I started with twelve-minute walks. Before long, I was walking for thirty minutes. It is very important to keep moving.

One major thing I learned was that I had to work at recovery daily and much of it was hard work. I had to push myself to stay on track sometimes, especially in the early stages when I didn't feel like I was making any progress. Although, regaining my health was a priority, my thoughts and activities were focused on my family, my household, and all the myriads of activities to keep both going—with me in charge.

I can honestly say that I am doing everything I did before I had the cancer and probably more. I feel better because I exercise and take very good care of myself. I have a few restrictions on some activities and some foods, but they do not hamper my lifestyle. For example, I am not permitted to eat raw fish or meat—no problem for me on that one. I cannot swim in lakes because of the bacteria and I cannot have vaccines, so no flu shots. My immune system is selectively depressed to keep my body from rejecting my heart. As a result, it could be difficult to fight a bug.

The immune system immediately goes to work to eject something that it decides doesn't belong in the body it is protecting, whether it is a splinter, a cold, flu, or a transplanted organ. My immune system cannot discern that my heart is a good thing so will always try to tell it to leave my body. However, as time goes on, it does become more accepting. Selectively depressing my immune system to keep it from rejecting my heart makes me more susceptible to infection. Therefore, I am cautious when I am around sick people.

My visits to the medical center have diminished. After the first year, it tapers off. I take about twenty-five pills a day still but it has become such a part of my life that I do not even think of it. In fact, once in awhile, I forget when I'm away from home. It is hard to remember to take medicine when you are not sick. I no longer fear rejection. Oh, I've had my share of rejection episodes but it has been detected in biopsies so it has been treated before I showed any outward symptoms. Treatment is an adjustment in the anti-rejection medications with follow-up blood tests and a biopsy to assure that it is under control. It is important to treat it in the early stages before it becomes a major problem. The warning signs of rejection are similar to other ailments such as the flu so I need to be conscientious about keeping in touch with Celia and Anne, the heart transplant coordinators. I've learned not to let minor rejection episodes upset me; I adjust my medicine and get on with my life.

I've had my ups and downs including slight rejections, pneumonia, skin cancer, a punctured lung, and hot flashes for six years but they were minor problems in the total scheme. I'm sure any one of those ailments would have been major if I hadn't experienced breast cancer, a mastectomy, chemotherapy, heart failure, and a heart transplant. It is true that everything is relative.

There is a certain sense of loneliness in all of this. No matter how many people stand by your bedside, love and support you, you have to go through it alone. No one rolls into the MRI with you; no one gets millions of needle sticks with you; no one is on the table with you when you have your biopsy; no one has x-ray after x-ray with you, no one walks with you on the treadmill or blows with you in the pulmonary function tests or lies with you under those huge cameras in nuclear medicine.

People often ask how I got through it. I grew up in a large Irish Catholic family where a sense of humor was important and there was no feeling sorry for oneself. I never considered myself athletic or a physically strong person, but I've learned that I do have an inner strength. I tried to be cheerful and never complain even when I was at the bottom of the barrel. I knew no one wanted to be around a grumpy patient. I took one step at a time, not one day or one hour. Sometimes, it had to be minutes. Having something, anything, to look forward to helped me. It could be a visit from Bill, completing a test, lunch, reading a magazine, etc. Also, I have a large extended family and many, many, marvelous, caring friends. Their encouraging notes, cards, and prayers were a major contribution to my survival.

My very special mother-in-law came to our house every day to make sure everything was in order and to be there when Shannon and Brendan arrived home from school. She organized the household chores and made sure dinner was arranged and everything was tidy when Bill came home from work. She did much more that I learned about later. It was amazing how she ran two households simultaneously. I'm sure she gave up many of her own activities to help us. Jennie popped in almost daily to see how my mother-in-law was doing. Friends brought dinner in regularly and helped with the children. I could write a book about the nice things people did for us that made it easier for all of us to cope. With their support and prayers, we made it from start to finish including a happy ending.

Do I stop and smell the roses? My life has definitely been affected by my experience but my values haven't changed. My family has always been the most important thing to me and that is still true. I have no feeling of urgency about doing and experiencing things I haven't done although I am very aware of how quickly life can change. I do not dwell on that possibility.

Sometimes, when I look at something ahead of me that I think will be stressful or difficult, I say to myself, "Good grief, it is not as bad as having a heart transplant. This is a snap." I then plow ahead more relaxed.

My family and friends are more important to me than ever. I've asked my family and several friends if they think I have changed. Always, the answer is an emphatic, "No." I don't think they're kidding me; I don't think that I have changed either. It is just the same "me" with an added experience and a young heart.

The possibility of a recurring cancer, heart failure, rejection, or serious medicine side effects still hang over my head but I don't dwell on them. I try to keep all of this in perspective remembering something my mother used to say, "Everybody gets something." I caught myself thinking of little sayings she said to me over the years. They would come back out of the blue; it helped me cope with this overwhelming experience. I imagine I'm doing the same with my children. That is how philosophies get passed from one generation to another. Somehow, I feel as if I've had my share, but I'm always semi-prepared for bad news. Having survived this medical adventure, I'm almost certain I can handle anything that comes my way. Should I have any more major medical problems, my hope is that I can handle them with dignity.

This is not meant to be a sob story nor should it frighten anyone who might now be going through chemotherapy. Medicine has made great strides which should help present recipients of chemotherapy. What happened to me, happens to one in a million, literally. With improved drugs, administration of therapy, and medical supervision, this should not recur.

I have no resentment or bitterness. When I recall that my perfectly healthy heart was unnecessarily damaged by chemotherapy, I put it behind me. Realizing how very lucky I am to have a new heart and a new life, I look to the future.

Recently, I had an experience that made my heart jump for joy. I was departing from the Raleigh, North Carolina airport on my way to visit my family in Indiana. I always carry my medications with me rather than check them through with my luggage. Just in case my luggage would be lost or delayed, I could be in trouble because I am dependent on my pills. Plopping my bag on the security belt, I quickly slipped through the metal detector. As I reached for my carry-on bag, the security guard grabbed it and asked, "Do you mind if I open this?"

"Not at all," I answered as I mentally searched the bag trying to imagine what was in there that would trigger his interest.

He immediately picked out the plastic pouch that contained all my medications. I had a two-week supply of pills which were separated into those weekly dispensers. The guard looked at them and then looked up at me and said, "Do you take all these?"

Not wanting to cause a scene and raise his suspicion anymore, I confidently replied, "Yes, I have had a heart transplant." Quickly, I tried to think how I could prove it if this scene escalated.

He looked inside the pouch again and looked at me and declared, "You don't look like you have had a heart transplant."

I smiled. "This is what a heart transplant looks like."

He firmly zipped my bag, handed it to me and sent me on my way with a final comment, "Take care of yourself."

Walking away on cloud nine, I called out, "Thanks a million." He didn't know it but he made my day.

Chapter Fourteen

Would the Tears Ever Stop?

My children are the sunshine in my life, part of my living being. When each was born, it was an instant love affair. Every day, I get more attached to them. I look forward to hearing their voices, seeing their smiling faces—even their frowning ones. I love spending time with them. Each is unique, interesting, and good company. I enjoy their journey into adulthood as I watch them mature and try their wings with all the normal bumps along the way. I glow with pride when I think of their achievements.

There is always a little part of me that worries about their safety and can always focus on the hazard in any situation. I worry about their health too because I can always recall a story about someone's child who had a major medical problem that changed their families' lives. The children's hospitals are full of those girls and boys. My heart aches for them and their families—even more so now that I have had a catastrophic illness. And in the back of my mind is the always lingering fear that except for the grace of God, one of my children could be there.

The death of a child must be one of life's worst agonies. I'm not even going to pretend that I know how badly it hurts. I can't imagine anything worse; it is almost impossible to contemplate. Whenever the thought of it enters my mind, I quickly chase it out. My heart chokes when I think of parents who have experienced the death of a child.

Since I was given the chance to keep living because someone's son died is a dichotomy that continues to occupy my thoughts. I think of his family and how their lives were probably going along routinely with activities revolving around family life when suddenly it was all taken out from under them. I'm sure their hearts were crushed into millions of pieces permeating their whole beings. To think that at the moment of a tragic, unplanned death of a child they could even think about another family who was going through a similar situation is phenomenal. I am overwhelmed they would give such a generous gift to someone they didn't know who had a thread of hope to live with an organ transplant. There is no "thank you" large enough to express my eternal gratitude to them.

Hopefully, with time, they have healed although I know the pain would never go away. Would it ease their sorrow knowing a part of their child lives on and is doing well? Would the tears ever stop? I don't know; I can't imagine. Do they get solace from memories? Would it help to know I celebrate his life on the anniversary of my transplant every year? Is it in some small way consoling to know their son doesn't have to face the negatives in the world? Do they often think of the special things they have been robbed of, like grandchildren? Are they frequently reminded of things they did with their son? Are they bitter? I don't think so because they thought of another dying person when they were experiencing undescribable emptiness and ache.

Their son is in my thoughts all the time especially since he would have been just a few years older than my children. I'm sure they have the same wonders about him as I do. Would he have graduated from college by now? Would he have fallen in and out of love and perhaps broken some hearts along the way? What career path would he have taken? What would he look like as an adult? Would he have a wife and maybe a baby? Would it be consoling to know that someone else is thinking of him too? I hope so . . . because I do.

Chapter Fifteen

Every Day Is a Gift

When I look back on this seven-month medical journey that included breast cancer, a mastectomy, chemotherapy, heart failure and a heart transplant, I shake my head and think how lucky I am to be alive.

Sometimes, I think more families would donate organs from their loved ones if they could see the impressive results and how they give another person a second chance at life. Most of us are average, everyday citizens, are not sickly and lead normal, active lives. We are of all ages, backgrounds and come from all cultures.

The waiting lists for organs are long; many die waiting. In our country, every two hours someone dies waiting for the gift of an organ. Research shows that families are better prepared to donate if they have discussed their wishes in advance. It only takes a few minutes.

When I was a teenager, a solicitation arrived in the mail from the Living Bank which was recruiting members to agree to organ donation. I read all the literature and completed the forms and the card. My parents witnessed my signature and until recently, I carried that withered old card in my wallet. Never, ever, ever did I dream I would be on the other side someday—receiving the gift of an organ. My driver's license now has the pink donor dot on it and my family knows of my wishes.

I am so fortunate. I take care of my new heart, faithfully keeping the promises required of each recipient to follow the strict medical regime for the rest of my life span.

My Dad used to say, "Every day is a gift." He was right.

Mom's Diary, December 31, 1989

In summarizing this year, I can truthfully say it was the most stressful year I've had since Bill [my dad] died. Nancy's illness was a shock and brought us all closer together as a family. We realized how many good friends we had, what prayers could do and how grateful we all are to God to have spared Nancy's life. No matter what her life span may be—we are grateful she was spared at this time. It showed all of us what a truly good man Bill Pedder is—a good husband and a great dad. His parents gave Nancy and Bill great support and courage—an added blessing. To me, all my other five children proved they were true blue and would help any of the others in the family who needed help or in any other emergency. So as I move into another decade, and look back, I realize what a great blessing I enjoyed in my family. I'm losing some of my physical skills and compensating for them as much as I can and I am grateful for good health which I enjoyed most of this year. No one knows what the future holds but I'm

confident I am ready to meet it cheerfully. I close
the book on 1989.

Mary A. Shank

December 31, 1989

Epilogue

Although the telling of my story is meant to demonstrate the positive side of transplantation and encourage organ donors, it began with breast cancer. Early detection did save my life too. I urge all women to be faithful about self-examination and regular mammograms. Evelyn Lauder, senior vice president of Estee Lauder and founder of The Breast Cancer Research Foundation recently said, "One hundred and ninety thousand women are diagnosed with breast cancer each year; 44,000 die; 19,000 (of those) lives could have been saved if they'd practiced early detection techniques. Knowledge is power" (San Francisco Chronicle, 1997, p. E7).

Now that I have shared part of my life with you, I hope you understand that you can be part of this great gift of life for another person by signing a donor card. In addition to organs, many other parts of the body such as bone, corneas, and skin can be used to help someone else.

It is important to think about this in advance and discuss it with family members so in case of injury or sickness, your family will know of your wishes to be a donor. No other action can compare with the satisfaction of realizing that you made life possible for another dying person.

Thank you.

Nancy Pedder

Facts about Organ and Tissue Donation

♡ A donated organ can save the life of a patient who, for example, has heart or liver disease. A new pancreas may cure diabetes. Bone marrow can combat leukemia and skin grafts help prevent infection in burn victims. Bones can prevent the amputation of an arm or a leg, strengthen fractured bones and be used in hip revisions, spinal fusions, and oral and facial reconstructions. A new cornea can correct failing eyesight and the small bones housed in the middle ear may be used to repair a hearing deficit.

♡ More than 50,000 people currently are waiting for organ transplants in the United States. A new name is added to the national waiting list every 18 minutes.

♡ Nationally, one person dies every two hours because of the critical shortage.

♡ The need for donor organs continues to surpass the supply.

♡ Transplantation is no longer considered experimental. It is a desired treatment for thousands with end-stage organ disease.

♡ Current medical technology allows the transplantation of skin, cornea, bone, bone marrow, blood, kidneys, heart, lung, pancreas, liver, heart valves, cartilage, tendons, fascia, and dura.

♡ A single organ and tissue donor can benefit more than fifty people.

♡ Donation is a sterile surgical procedure. Open casket funerals are possible.

♡ Organ donation and transplantation are consistent with the life preserving traditions of most major religious groups in the United States. Most religions approve and support the principles and practices of organ and tissue donation.

♡ Donor families incur no expense for donation. They do not pay for, nor receive payment for, organ and tissue donation. Hospital expenses incurred before the donation of organs and funeral expenses remain the responsibility of the donor's family. All costs related to donation are paid for by the organ procurement organization or transplant center.

♡ Organ donation is considered only after all life-saving options have failed. A transplant team does not become involved until the patient's primary care physicians have determined that all possible efforts to save the patient's life have failed.

♡ Donation does not take place until the patient has met the criteria of brain death.

♡ A person who is brain dead has suffered a severe head injury such as an accident, stroke or hemorrhage or prolonged lack of oxygen to the brain. There are specific tests to determine brain death approved by the American Medical Association. More than half of the donors have non-traumatic causes of brain death, such as brain aneurysms and strokes.

♡ Brain death and coma are different. A person in a coma has brain activity and therefore may regain consciousness.

♡ About five out of one hundred deaths are brain deaths.

♡ Besides a brain that is not functioning, other criteria for potential organ and tissue donors include certain age limits and the absence of unresolved systemic infections or extra-cerebral malignancies. The average age of a donor is 38 years.

♡ The Uniform Anatomical Gift Act of 1968 insures that organ recovery is efficient and that donated organs are distributed equitably. It also prohibits physicians who declare death from participating in recovery or transplant procedures.

♡ The medical staff does not lower its quality of care if it knows of the patient's wishes to become a donor.

♡ Candidates who are awaiting organ transplants must match the donor's size and blood group. They must be healthy enough to undergo major surgery and willing to be transplanted immediately.

♡ In allocating organs and tissue donation, the Donor Network considers the candidate's medical condition, length of time on the waiting list, and immune status. Preference is not given to a wealthy or well-known patient. How far the potential recipient is from the donor hospital is taken into consideration for heart, heart-lung, liver, lung, and pancreas transplants.

♡ The National Organ Transplant Act of 1984 prohibits the sale and purchase of human organs.

♡ Experience shows that families are more willing to donate if they have discussed donation with the deceased. Because consent from the next-of-kin is required, family members who are unaware of their loved one's wishes are less likely to consent to donation.

♡

♡ There is no national registry of those who have indicated their willingness to be organ and tissue donors.

♡ Donor families say that donation helps them to heal. Knowing they have fulfilled their loved one's wishes and have helped another person by saving their life or improving their health makes their tragedy a little more bearable. It gives them a feeling of peace and comfort.

♡ An Organ Procurement Organization is the link between potential donors and individuals awaiting organ and tissue transplantation. For more information, call 800-55-DONOR.

♡ How can you help save lives? Make a commitment to learn the facts about organ and tissue donation. Decide to become a donor. Discuss your wishes with your family.

Source: California Transplant Donor Network

Resources

Transplant Society (TS)
SUNY at Stony Brook, Dept. of Surgery
Health Science Center
Stony Brook, NY 11794-8192
(516) 444-2209

United Network for Organ Sharing (UNOS)
1100 Boulders Pky, #500
PO Box 13770
Richmond, VA 23225
(804) 330-8500

International Transplant Nurses Society (ITNS)
Foster Plaza Blvd 5
651 Holiday Dr. #300
Pittsburgh, PA 15220-2740
(412) 928-3667

Center for Organ Recovery & Education (CORE)
204 Sigma Drive
Ride Park
Pittsburgh, PA 15238
(800) 366-6777

North American Transplant Coordinators Organization (NATCO)
PO Box 15384
Lenexa, KS 66285-5384
(913) 492-3600

Organ Transplant Fund
1102 Brookfield, Suite 202
Memphis, TN 38119
National Director: Gary L. McMahan
(800) 489-3863

Transplant Recipients International Organization (TRIO)
1000 16th Street, NW, #602
Washington, DC 20036-5705
(202) 293-0980

American Medical Association
515 N. State Street
Chicago, IL 60610
(312) 464-5000

Life Banc
20600 Chagrin Blvd #350
Cleveland, OH 44122-5343
Ex. Director: Kristine Nelson, RN HN
(216) 752-5433
(800) 558-5433

American Heart Association
7272 Greenville Ave
Dallas, TX 75231-4596
Ex. Vice President: Dudley H. Hafner
(214) 373-6300
(800) 742-1793

American Society of Transplant Surgeons (ASTS)
716 Lee Street
Des Plaines, IL 60016
Janet H. Wright, Adm.
(847) 824-5700

Nicholas Green Foundation
PO Box 937
Bodega Bay, CA 94923
Founders: Reginald and Maggie Green

National Coalition on Organ and Tissue Donation
(800) 355-7427

WEB SITES

♡ Organ Transplant Fund, Inc.
www.otf.org

♡ All About Transplantation and Donation
www.transweb.org

♡ Nicholas Green Foundation
www.greenfoundation.com

♡ www.shareyourlife.org

♡ www.organdonor.gov

ORGAN AND TISSUE DONATION GUIDELINES

Organ	Age Limits	Application
Heart	Newborn to 60	End stage heart disease
Heart/Lung	Newborn to 60	End stage cardiopulmonary disease
Heart Valves	3 months to 55	Valve replacement
Kidney	1 month to 70	End stage renal disease
Liver	Newborn to 65	End stage liver disease
Pancreas	7 years to 55	Diabetes mellitus

Tissue	Age Limits	Application
Bone	15 to 65	Iliac crest and femurs processed into dowels, blocks and chips for use in spinal fusions and non-union fractures
Costal Cartilage	15 to 35	Used for facial reconstruction
Dura Mater	15 to 55	Used for surgical repairs of head injuries and reconstruction of middle ear
Eye	5 to 70	Corneal transplantation
	Newborn to 5 and over 70	Medical research and training
Heart Valves	3 months to 55	Valve replacement
Fascia Lata	15 to 55	Same applications as dura
Middle Ear	15 to 55	Used to repair hearing deficits
Skin	15 to 55	Used as a dressing for third degree burns
Tendons and ligaments	15 to 45	Sports injury repairs

Only eye donations are accepted from patients with a history of metastatic cancer.

Untreated systemic infection may preclude donation.

Organ donation can only take place when a patient has met criteria of brain death; the patient's vital signs must be supported until the organ recovery takes place.

The eyes must be removed within 6 to 8 hours after death; all other tissues can be removed within 24 hours of death.

About the Author

Born the oldest of six children, Nancy Shank Pedder was raised in Indianapolis, Indiana. She graduated from Purdue University and currently resides in Oakland, California with her husband of thirty years and their two children. She has been a full-time mother and community volunteer. Nancy is an inspirational speaker and talks to groups about organ donation and transplantation. She enjoys her friends, her investment and garden clubs, reading, swimming, walking, traveling and has recently rekindled her painting career.